The Psychotherapy Workbook

The Psychotherapy Workbook

A Home-Study Guide For Growth & Change

FIRST EDITION

Kathleen Cairns, Psy. D.

 **LIFE GOES ON PRODUCTIONS**

Publisher's Note

This publication is meant to provide accurate information on the topic of psychotherapy. It is sold with the understanding that the author is not engaged in giving psychological services to the reader. If individual assistance or psychotherapy is needed, a competent professional should be sought.

The Psychotherapy Workbook
Copyright © 1997 Kathleen Cairns

Published by:
Life Goes On Productions
Post Office Box 18380
Beverly Hills, California 90209
tel 310.858.7474
fax 310.246.9545
e-mail lifegoeson@earthlink.net

ISBN 1-891409-00-X Paperback

Cover & graphic design by Dorrie Cheng.

Printed in the United States of America on recycled paper.

FIRST EDITION

I dedicate this book to my parents, Thomas & Helen Cairns,
who gave me loving Programs.
Thank you very much.

I wish to express my gratitude to

my patients, for sharing their journeys of growth and change with me.

Barry Fox, Ph.D., for teaching me how to write a book.

Lyn & Norman Lear, for opening their beautiful home to the Kindred Spirits.

Harold Bloomfield, M.D. and his beautiful wife Sirah Vettese, Ph.D., for their help and kindness.

Lynn Ludlam, for her encouragement and belief in my writing.

Toni Lopopolo, for introducing me to Sol Stein.

Sandra Fenster, Ph.D., for introducing me to myself.

Barbara Barnett, Ph.D., my colleague and friend, for her love and wisdom over the years.

Anna Thompson, for twenty-five years of best-friendship.

Gracie, my little assistant, for her playful soul.

Linda, my sister, for her amazing ideas and generous praise.

Stephen, my nowever husband, for his loving heart, and

my parents, for giving me everything I need.

TABLE OF CONTENTS

The Stories

"The great man is he who does not lose his child's heart."

Mencius, Works 327-289 B.C.

"Children begin by loving their parents; as they grow older they judge them; sometimes they forgive them."

Oscar Wilde, from the Preface of "The Picture of Dorian Gray" 1891

Introduction - From Freud To Geraldo

We want to stop the pain. We want to fill the gaping hole we sense is deep inside of us. We look outside for love, attention, money, power, control, and validation. We don't feel our own completeness, wholeness, and perfection.

No longer willing to suffer in silence like good little victims, we are now talking. Endlessly. Witness the success of television shows such as "Oprah," "Leeza," "Sally Jessie Raphael," and "Montel Williams." Freud initiated this "talking cure" in the beginning of the twentieth century. From Freud to "Geraldo" in just a few decades.

In the old days, doctors were men and women in the community who were religious and spiritual healers. Shamans, priests, wise men, and gifted women with magic potions. There was a "magical covenant," an unspoken contract of faith and trust in the healing powers of the mystical authority figure. The success of the healing depended on the shared belief system of the patient and the community, the idealization of the healer, and the healer's belief in himself. This paradigm lasted for thousands of years, and still exists in certain cultures.

To a large extent, the spirituality of today's New Age movement may be seen as a renewed interest and respect for ancient inner healing techniques. Homeopathy, acupuncture, naturopathy, aromatherapy, hydrotherapy, hands-on healing, chiropractic, chakra alignment, psychic readings, astrology, channeling, past-life regression. The list goes on. There is a global interest in ancient means of healing and cure. We see a renewed religious movement reflected by the large number of trans-denominational churches in this country. But psychological healing is relatively new. Modern psychology is based on Freud's understanding of the relationship between patient and doctor, the magical release of pain through talking, and the notions of repression, denial, and motivation. His ideas gave rise to therapy as we know it today.

The therapist replaced the priest. The couch replaced the temple. Anti-depressants and tranquilizers replaced incense and herbs.

Let The Healing Begin

Our pain comes from childhood because our parents weren't perfect. They were human. We were injured in childhood but we still feel the pain as adults. And what is our pain? The pain is *fear*; the fear that we're not good enough, not lovable, not special, not whole. We hide from who we really are, hoping not to see our flaws, our ugliness, our vulnerability. And with fear comes the imprisonment of our souls. We lock away our true selves, and present a false mask to the world, a mask we think is more lovable, more worthy of acceptance and love. But we're wrong. The true self, the better self, is locked away; unfree, waiting to be wanted and missed, but not knowing how to reappear.

Baby Boomers are rather intolerant of pain and depression. We are endlessly looking for relief in the form of a magic pill, a quick remedy, or a new guru. The search is expanding into our world view as well. Evolving politics are calling for freedom on every continent. Witness the end of apartheid in South Africa, the fall of the Wall in Berlin, and the end of Communism.

We are demanding freedom for ourselves, for our community, and for our world. At the turn of the 21st century, the 90's have been as free and evolutionary as the 60's. Now is the time to free and heal our true psychological selves.

Parental Programs

In this Workbook, I offer a metaphor for healing: ***The Parental Program***. Just like programmers input software and data into the hard drive of a computer, our parents "program" our self-concept by their words and actions. Parental Programs are messages we receive in childhood telling us who we are. As a computer obeys the commands in its programs, we obey the commands in our unconscious minds. Our parents supply the data with words: *"You're just like your father!" "You're stupid." "You're pretty."* And with actions: Absence and neglect makes us feel unimportant. Drinking makes us scared. Yelling tells us we're bad. Love makes us feel worthy. If we *think* we're unworthy, we'll sabotage ourselves. If we *feel* stupid, we won't even try. Unconscious Negative Parental Programs hinder our freedom to live happily and to have successful relationships and jobs.

Bad Programs, Not Bad Parents

It has become fashionable in the past few decades to analyze, blame, and judge parents for all of our problems. But I believe we can heal in a much more loving way by replacing blame and judgment with understanding and compassion.

There are many good, kind, loving, respectful, supportive parents who give wonderful Programs to their children. I want to make it clear that no one is all bad or all good. Mother Teresa probably had some annoying habits, while Hitler's charisma led a nation to destruction.

In this Workbook, I am focusing on Negative Programs. My patients who have stories of abuse also have memories of tender moments with the same parent. I'm not writing about blame. I'm writing about understanding. When you read the stories, please read them with compassion for the abusive parent. He or she received Negative Programs from the Grandfather or Grandmother of the patient, who had received Negative Programs from the Great-Grandfather or Great-Grandmother of the patient, and on and on...

No one is born evil or abusive.

The Stories

We are all fascinated with each other. We're intrigued by the human condition. In books and movies, we seek entertainment and comfort by watching other people's lives because we want to understand the deeper meaning within our own. In reading about the rich and famous, we become so involved, we often feel we know them. Remember how the world shared a collective loss at the death of Princess Diana, having watched her story-book life of not only fame and beauty, but of insecurity and bulimia. We saw a real woman with real problems, and we loved her for her vulnerability. If people we like have weakness and pain, it must be OK for us to be less than perfect too. It is for this reason that I have written the case histories in this book. The stories are about everyday people with everyday problems and everyday lives. We can identify with them, and learn from their growth and change.

With case studies, I illustrate the acting out of Parental Programs by men and women of all ages and backgrounds. The people you will read about have all been patients of mine at one time. I've changed the names and identifying information, but have kept true to the essence of each person to the best of my ability. I am truly grateful for their willingness to allow me into their lives.

Your Story

We are all vulnerable to the dictates of Programs, regardless of socio-economic background, race, religion, or gender. My hope is that in reading these case histories, you may recognize your own Programs. Once seen, you are then free to decide if they are appropriate for you today.

In coming chapters we'll explore ways of discovering your own Programs. Do you like your Programs? Do they make your life happy, fulfilling, rewarding? Are you free to be yourself? Would you like to erase your old Programs and write them anew?

This Workbook is intended to be a home-study guide for growth and change, as if you were a patient of mine. Together, we will uncover your Programs. We will look inside, find your pain, and begin the journey. Hopefully, it will set you free.

Throughout this Workbook, we will see how Programs we received in childhood have long-lasting effects throughout our lives. We learn who we are with the mind of a child, blindly accepting our Programs for the rest of our lives. It's time to analyze these self-definitions. *Are they true? Do they accurately portray our true selves? Or are we more, better, smarter, nicer, more loving, more successful, than we have been led to believe?*

If the Negative False Programs are the flaws, we now have the software to cure ourselves. We can identify our negative ideas about ourselves, see ourselves through clear, adult eyes for the first time, *and decide who we really are.*

Identifying your Programs

Now imagine you are my patient. You got my name from a trusted friend, teacher, advisor, or physician. You made the decision to try psychotherapy. You called me, and we arranged a time for our first appointment. You felt a little scared, nervous, and curious. Upon entering my waiting room, you noticed there were no magazines, nothing to distract you from your own feelings and thoughts. I opened the door to my office, invited you in, and the process began.

I want you to continue to imagine this as you let this Workbook be your **Home-Study Guide For Growth and Change.** Allow yourself to personally go through the stages of therapy as you read each chapter. As you read the Stories, take the Questionnaires, and do the Exercises and Homework, notice the self-discoveries along the way and write them on the *Insight* pages at the end of each chapter. Whether you're already in therapy, contemplating therapy, or simply want to go through the process of therapy with this Workbook alone, allow this experience to help you free your true self.

Questionnaires, Exercises, and Homework

In every chapter, there are Questionnaires, Exercises, and Homework to help you reprogram your software, replacing negativity and restrictions with positivity and freedom. They are designed to help you uncover your Programs, reveal your true self, and be free to live the life you deserve. The Questionnaires begin the process of remembering your past, and the Homework assignments guide you to continue your growth and change in the future. The Exercises give you constructive and tangible activities to change your unconscious beliefs and behaviors. All of this can be done privately, at your own pace, whenever you are ready. It's important to do them in the order they are presented. One at a time, one chapter at a time. Fill out each Questionnaire slowly, with concentration and thought. Participate in each Exercise thoroughly, with willingness to explore your Self. Let the Homework be creative and fun. Some activities will be more fitting for you than others. Remember, the more you give, the more you will receive.

And the healing will begin.

"If a man has been his mother's undisputed darling he retains throughout life the triumphant feeling, the confidence in success, which not seldom brings actual success with it."

Freud, from "A Childhood Memory of Goethe's" 1917

"The computer is no better than its program."

Elting Elmore Morison, from "Men, Machines, and Modern Times" 1966

Chapter 1

Parental Programs: Your Internal Drive

The Beautiful Vase

Imagine a beautiful a vase, brilliant in color, perfect in design. See water being poured into the vase. But this vase has a hole. Not a large hole, but big enough to allow the water to seep out the bottom. Pour in more water and it merely flows out. We repeat this pouring in of more water until it finally occurs to us that the solution is not more water. *The answer lies in repairing the hole.*

We are the vase. The water is external things that we think make us happy; relationships, love, money, houses, cars, drugs, or alcohol. The hole is our injured self-esteem. We can attempt to make ourselves complete and happy by using people and things. We can pour in more water. But we won't be able to hold onto these things; we won't be able to believe we really deserve them. It's only when we repair our sense of self that we can have meaning in our lives, that we can feel loved and whole. So how do we do this? What's the answer to the eternal question, *"How can I learn to love myself?"*

Unhappy relationships caused by a lack of self-love are the most common problems people bring to a therapist's office. Although couples argue over money and children and whether the toilet seat should be left up or down, the real problem is that we feel our needs aren't being met, and we don't know what we need. Our sense of deservedness and self-esteem is low. We have minimal tools for coping with this lack of satisfaction in our lives. We are afraid.

When we are newly born babies, we're full of love and openness. We're so filled with love for ourselves and others, we're aware of little else. So where do we learn that we're not good enough, not lovable, not worthy, not deserving of love? When were we infected with the virus of self-doubt?

Tracking Down The Virus

We are infected when we cry as a child but no one comforts us. We are infected when we hurt and want to be held but are instead ignored or punished. We are infected when our parents misinterpret our needs. We are infected when an impatient or drunk caretaker beats us. We are infected when we are sexually abused by a parent who was himself sexually abused. We are infected when we are told we are stupid or a failure or ugly or useless or bad or in the way. We are infected when we learn negative things about ourselves in a context of neglect, abuse, or ignorance.

Patients who come to my office all have self-definitions based on what they were taught at the moment of infection. If a child was beaten by an alcoholic parent, he is infected with the germ of unlovableness: *"If I were more lovable, my father would not drink. He beats me because I am bad."* The child doesn't have the intellect or maturity to see that the father has a disease. If a child is neglected by a workaholic, she's infected by the germ of unworthiness: *"If I were worthy of time and attention, my mother would come home earlier and spend time with me. I am not good enough."* The little girl doesn't have the insight to understand that the real problem is the workaholic's need to over-function and escape on the job.

Parental Programs

Our minds and spirits are impressionable when we're young, easily influenced by every person and event in our world. Parents are god-like creatures who hold our lives in their hands and seem to know everything. We believe everything they say, pay attention to everything they do. We look to them to tell us who we are: good or bad, stupid or smart, pretty or ugly, worthy or undeserving, important or insignificant. They tell us who we are with their words and more often by their behaviors. I call these words and behaviors "**Programs**".

Parental Program is a term I have coined to describe the unconscious "orders for life" we receive from our parental figures. Our parents teach us who we are by how they behave towards us and how they treat us, thus giving us our self-definitions. We carefully and unquestioningly obey and execute these definitions of self at all costs, *even when doing so is painful and counter-productive.*

We all have Programs, most of them given to us by our parents when we were very young. Additional Programs are given to us by aunts, uncles, siblings, teachers, or authority figures. Our Programs tell us who we *must* be, how we *must* behave, and how we *must* think of ourselves. We carefully and unquestioningly obey and execute these Programs, even when we know our behavior is self-destructive. ***Every Program must be obeyed.***

If we are soothed when we cry, we eagerly accept the Positive Parental Program that says we're worthy, deserving, and lovable. If we're beaten or ignored, we just as impressionably accept the Negative Parental Program that insists we're unworthy, undeserving, and unlovable. These Programs become our life-long beliefs. They're irrefutable facts. If we had an abusive childhood, if we "learned" we're unworthy, undeserving, and unlovable, it's difficult to "unlearn" this as adults, no matter how much evidence to the contrary is heaped before our eyes. We've all met wonderfully lovable adults who have low self-esteem, whose Programs won't let them believe they're worthy, deserving, talented, or lovable. We can meet hundreds of people in our adult lives who tell us we're wonderful, but we only believe the Programs we received from a handful of people when we were children. We believe them for life. *But, we can begin to change when we recognize the Programs.*

A beautiful baby

Imagine a child is born. A beautiful baby. This baby is created and brought into this world feeling completely open and loving toward himself and everyone in the world, arms and heart open wide. But his parents are human, which means they aren't perfect. They have their own hurts and shortcomings. And when they aren't able to perfectly meet the baby's needs, he is hurt. And in his childhood, he will experience other disappointments, hurtful words and actions, and unmet needs. He then learns to defend against the pain. He becomes fearful and closes his arms and his heart. The beautiful baby creates a mask to wear, a false outer-self that protects him. And the masks, the defenses, and the Negative Programs are passed down from generation to generation.

No one is born evil or abusive. Hate and fear are masks we wear, the outer manifestations of our Negative Programs. Our goal in this lifetime is to get rid of our masks and false selves, to once again accept ourselves for who and what we are, and to return to who we were at the time of our birth: *all good, all kind, all loving.*

Children believe what their parents tell them about themselves in word and deed. Forever, subtly, unconsciously. It's only when we go back to the scene of the infection and discover *how* we learned our negative Programs that we can begin to free ourselves of their harmful effects. Only then are we free to become who we were truly meant to be.

Computer Programs

I use the analogy of computer programs because computers have become a common yet tremendous influence in our lives. We have changed the way our children learn in school. We write letters and books at the keyboard, taking for granted the amazing mechanism that cuts and pastes and deletes at the touch of a key. We know the computer can only obey commands that have been installed on the hard drive or on the floppy disk. Despite our frustrations, we've learned that if something goes wrong, it's our fault. The computer can't make its own changes, nor can it program itself. We are like the hard drive. We receive Programs from our parents, siblings, and other significant people in our childhood. And like computers, we are obliged to obey these "commands" until we uncover them and decide to keep them or delete them. *But most of us never realize that we can change and rewrite our Programs.*

Imagine Parental Program software. Every time a parent interacts with a child, a Program is written and "installed" into the child. When we feel a tender touch, it's as if our parents give us a Program that says: *"You are loved and lovable."* When our parents speak to us with undue harshness, it's as if they install a Program that says: *"You are annoying and bad."*

And so it's with the same unquestioning faith that a child believes his parents' definition of who he is and how he should live his life. If a child is fortunate enough to have loving, nurturing parents, he will have good self-esteem (self-love). He'll know he's worthy, deserving, lovable, and safe. However, if a child is raised by a dysfunctional parent (unavailable, abusive, neglectful), he'll have low self-esteem because his Programs will tell him he's unworthy, undeserving, unlovable, or unsafe.

The Scene of the Crime

The **Scene of the Crime** are the times in childhood when Negative Programs were installed, teaching us we are less than enough. The Scene of the Crime are the moments in childhood when the hole in the vase was made. They consist of simple events, words, or behaviors that made us feel not-good-enough, unloved, unworthy, or not special. We need to look at these Scenes, not to blame our caretakers, but to understand, with compassion, so that we may be healed. We need to find the Scene of the Crime so we can understand why we are the way we are. Pain doesn't go away if ignored. It hurts even more. We realize the old ways of pretending, denial, and overcompensating don't work. It's time to try a different strategy.

Psychotherapy is one method of repairing the hole. Together, you and the therapist locate the hole and mend it, slowly, and with love. Or, you can work by yourself, with the assistance of self-help books, groups, friends, and family. Choose whatever feels right for you. The goal is to actively *do something* to repair the vase.

Michael's Story

The behavior that saved you as a child is the very behavior that hurts you as an adult. Michael is a perfect example. When Michael was a little boy, he learned that if he stayed very quiet, passive, and obedient, he would be safe from his bad-tempered father's tirades. It saved him from the punishments that his outspoken brothers received.

Michael's Father's Programs:

"You are not good enough."
"You are too loud."
"You are more likable when you are quiet and not in my way."
"It is safer to stay quiet and passive."
"Do as your told."

His father's constant criticism taught Michael self-criticism. And when he grew up, he still believed he wasn't good-enough, and that no one wanted to hear what he had to say. He continued to behave in a quiet, passive, obedient manner, so much so, that it hurt his career. He was afraid to speak in meetings at work and felt unable to offer new ideas. He was perceived as non-motivated and unintelligent by his supervisors. Even when asked for his thoughts, Michael still couldn't bring himself to give his opinions, afraid they would be wrong or not-good-enough. The quiet, passive, obedient behavior that saved him from his father's temper was exactly the same behavior that hurt him in his job.

Instant Replay

There is a very important term in psychology called **repetition compulsion.**

We have an unconscious desire to place ourselves in situations that make us feel exactly as we did as a child. We are compelled to repeat past behaviors and feelings.

For example, if a child is raised by an alcoholic, there is a very good chance that she will grow up to marry an alcoholic. It would seem against the odds, given the pain and turmoil of an alcoholic home. You would think she would avoid it at all costs. But it is *because* she was raised in pain and turmoil that it doesn't seem so unusual or bad. It seems normal and somehow comfortable. After all, she knows the behaviors. She knows what to do and how to act around an alcoholic. So when her husband gets drunk, it feels normal to be in the role of caretaker. Not because she loves taking care of a drunken man, but because she's done it countless times before as a child. Now, imagine a woman *not* raised by an alcoholic parent is dating an alcoholic. She isn't familiar with drunken behavior. So when her date gets drunk, she feels uncomfortable and doesn't want to be around him. His behavior doesn't match what feels known and normal to her.

It's very important to understand how we were programmed in order to find our own repetition compulsions. Freud said our goal is to make the unconscious conscious. If we make our unconscious Programs conscious, their power is lessened.

Our goal is to understand how our problems today are repeating the problems in our childhood. We need to understand the Scene of the Crime, find our Negative Parental Programs, connect them to our behavior today, and write better New Self-Programs.

Ellen's Story

Ellen is a beautiful attorney with a very successful practice in San Francisco. She is intelligent, out-going, and has many friends. She has it all, except for the one thing she wants the most; a family of her own. Ellen has been in a painful relationship with a married man for the last two years. She guiltily clings to the hope that he will someday leave his wife and three children, but in her saner moments she knows it will never happen.

When Ellen was a little girl, she jealously longed for the attention her younger brother received from her parents. He was born with a rare blood disease and required constant medical and parental attention. As a little girl, Ellen wasn't capable of understanding that her parents were over-wrought with worry for their son. All she knew was that she wasn't getting the attention she needed. As a little girl, she didn't have the ability to interpret her parents' behavior as necessary, under the circumstances. Little Ellen simply felt neglected. When she wanted her mother to read to her or play with her, her mother's answer was often *"I can't. I have to take care of your brother."*

Ellen's Parental Programs:

"You are second-best."
"You are not as important or lovable as your brother."
"You are not worthy of attention."

And so she unconsciously made her Programs true. She became involved in a relationship with a married man, someone whose attention would always be elsewhere. When she wanted to be with him on weekends and holidays, he wasn't available, for he chose to be with his family. As an adult, Ellen had as many lonely nights as she'd suffered through as a child. This relationship guaranteed she would always feel "second-best" and "not as important." *We are all unconsciously brilliant at making our Programs true, no matter how much it hurts.*

Maggie's Story

If our Program is to feel judged and criticized, we'll feel judgment and criticism from the outside world, even when no one is being critical. For example, twenty-eight year old Maggie once adopted an orphaned kitten. One day soon thereafter, the cat happened to be in the closet, watching her dress. Maggie, who had a long childhood history of negative criticism and judgment from her father, told me she *knew* the cat was looking at her critically, thinking *"You're not able to take care of me. You don't know what to do with me. You won't be a good mother."* This "criticism" made her feel inadequate and incapable. Obviously, the judgment wasn't coming from the cat; she was projecting her fears of being judged onto the cat. These thoughts were really coming from within Maggie from her old Programs.

Maggie's Parental Programs:

"You can't do anything right. "
"You are inadequate. "
"You are incapable."
"You can't be trusted with anything or anyone."
"You are a failure at everything."

Maggie kept finding ways to make her Programs come true, even when they were completely unfounded. *She needed those well-known, unhappy feelings, because they made her feel comfortable, in a very uncomfortable way.*

Our Programs drive our beliefs, our thoughts, and our actions. The only power strong enough to overcome a bad Program is a good Program. Only when the bad Programs have been driven out by good Programs are we able to write new self-definitions based on reality. Only then are we free to pursue relationships and careers based on our desires and abilities, not on our perceived limits and lack of confidence. But first we need to recognize our Negative Programs. We cannot begin to set ourselves free until we are aware of our blind beliefs in old Programs.

Your Turn

Now it's time to take your first step towards freedom. We begin with **Questionnaire 1: What's In Your Data Bank?** Answer quickly, without editing. Write what first comes into your mind. This questionnaire will jog your memory for **The "Parental Program" Exercise.** Take your time. It's the most important exercise in the Workbook. It provides you with the groundwork for self-understanding and change. And we end Chapter 1 with **Homework 1: Once Upon A Time..."** to remind you of your life so far.

Questionnaire 1

What's In Your Data Bank?

1. Describe your mother.

_____

_____

_____

_____

2. Describe your father.

_____

_____

_____

_____

3. Describe your siblings.

_____

_____

_____

_____

4. Describe other important adults in your childhood.

_____

_____

_____

_____

5. What were some of the adjectives your parents used to describe you?

_____

_____

_____

_____

6. How did they sound when they spoke to you?

_____

_____

_____

_____

_____

7. What do you remember about the atmosphere in your home?

_____

_____

_____

_____

8. Describe family dinner time.

_____

_____

_____

_____

9. What was your role in the family? Caretaker, peace-maker, clown?

_____

_____

_____

_____

_____

10. How did you feel about yourself at the age of three, four, five, and six?

_____

_____

_____

_____

11. Who are you now, in relation to your past identity?

_____

_____

_____

_____

_____

_____

_____

_____

_____

_____

The "Parental Program" Exercise

Purpose: * *To identify Negative Parental Programs*
                 * *To write New Positive Self Programs*

Let's look at the most important exercise first. I'll present a case history clearly illustrating the deep-rooted self-definitions that keep us from realizing our own potential. I will then show *The "Parental Program" Exercise* that will act as a guide when you do the exercise for yourself.

Greg's Story

Greg is a recovering cocaine addict referred by his mother with whom he lives. He works as an underpaid carpenter for an abusive employer. Greg's mother is classically co-dependent, taking care of Greg and her alcoholic husband and neglecting her own needs. She works full-time and is well loved in her community. She is the child of an alcoholic father. Greg's father spends most of his time with his drinking buddies, or at home in front of the television. He works sporadically.
In the initial session of therapy, it was clear Greg's self-esteem was very low, and his insight into his present circumstances was limited. We met five times before he could make eye contact with me. He perhaps expected me to somehow mistreat him too. Drinking and abuse were normal and comfortable for him. In his twenty-five years, he had never truly had a satisfying relationship.

"Nothing ever seems to work out for me. I never tried to do well in school because I felt stupid, and I always seemed to get into trouble. It just seemed to happen. I've tried to get better jobs, but I always seem to end up with a tyrant-type boss. I can't figure it out. I feel like such a loser. I haven't even had a real girlfriend before either. I think it's because I tried too hard. I was too nice, I guess. I'm sick of screwing up, and now that I've gotten a DUI, I've gotta change."

Not Good Enough

In looking closely at Greg's childhood, we discovered his father's Programs were *"You are not good enough. You will fail. You will never amount to anything or have anything."* This also appeared to be the father's own Program. Sometimes, Programs are multi-generational, handed down from father to son, on and on. His mother's Programs were *"Listen to your father (and therefore to his Programs). Let yourself be abused. I am the only one who really loves you."* The mother's own Parental Programs condoned her own abuse and neglect from her husband. She supported him with an old-fashioned *"Listen to your father; he is the head of the house."*

In the session where the Programs really came into focus, Greg's eyes widened with a look of *"That explains it!"* He said he was always late to school, that he tried to be on time, but he made himself be late *on purpose.*

"I could never understand why I would do this, but sometimes, when I was almost at school, I would make myself run back home so I would have to run back to school to try to be on time. And of course I'd be late. That always seemed like strange behavior to me, even at the time. That also explains why I stop trying when my volleyball team is about to win. I can feel myself stop trying when I can see we're gonna win. Even the guys on the team have noticed. It's weird. Do you mean that I've been doing this to myself just to make my father's Programs true?"

These are clear examples of making the Parental Programs true. Sometimes we sabotage ourselves repeatedly and never understand why. Sometimes we allow ourselves to have "just enough" of what we need, but never "too much." Sometimes we almost get what we want, only to lose it at the last moment. And we don't understand why this happens over and over again. Is it a coincidence we always end up in the same set of living circumstances? How is it we always seem to have the same lifestyle, always on the same level of comfort or discomfort, no matter what our job or where we live? We may call it "fear of success" or "fear of intimacy," but it all comes down to our obedience to our Programs.

In one of our first sessions together, I asked Greg to write out his Programs. I told him to list the Programs he received from his parents and other significant people, and to write how he made them come true.

FATHER'S PROGRAMS

You are a loser.
You can't do anything right.
You are not-good-enough.
You are a failure.
You are a screw-up.
You are stupid.
You are always in trouble.
You are worthless.
You are just like me.

HOW I MAKE THEM COME TRUE

I don't even try.
I quit when I'm close to success or winning, like in sports or school.
I make myself late.
I never studied. I mocked the smart kids. I thought of myself as dumb.
I took drugs to numb myself.
I abused my mind and body.
I drove after drinking and got a DUI.
I always work for bosses who exploit me. I let them exploit me.
I feel uncomfortable with someone who is nice to me.
I don't trust when people want to know me, like with girls.

MOTHER'S PROGRAMS

You deserve to be abused.
No one will ever love you except me.
You are helpless, weak, and a victim.
You are powerless.
It is your job to take care of everyone else before yourself.
You're just like your father.

HOW I MAKE THEM COME TRUE

I put myself in abusive situations (work, girlfriends, friends).
I am passive and take abuse.
I sabotage good things for myself.
I only go after girls who don't treat me well.
I'm uncomfortable around people who are nice to me.
I don't defend myself when I'm being yelled at.
I don't fight back.

TEACHERS' PROGRAMS

You're dumb because you're in the remedial class.
We don't expect much from you.

HOW I MAKE THEM COME TRUE

I never tried in school. I never studied.
I fooled around in class to get attention.

COACH'S PROGRAMS

You are a disappointment.
Every time we are close to winning, you slack off.
You don't want to win.
You never do your best.
We can't depend on you.

HOW I MAKE THEM COME TRUE

When we were close to winning,
I could feel myself losing the desire to win.
I felt uncomfortable being in the limelight.
I never tried my best.

Greg made all of his Programs come true. He caused trouble for himself in school, and kept himself from succeeding in sports. Thanks to his Parental Programs, he believed himself to be unlovable and felt he had to work extra hard to have a girlfriend, thereby sabotaging his relationships. He also believed himself to be worthy of abuse, so he naturally allowed himself to work under Dickinsonian circumstances.

Once he saw his Programs for defeat, he finally understood some of his negative behavior, and realized he needed Positive Self Programs to become healthy. During therapy, Greg was able to delete these Negative Programs and create his own Positive Programs for success, happiness, and love.

GREG'S NEW SELF PROGRAMS

I am a winner.
I am successful. I am smart.
I am assertive.
I am worthy of respect.
I am good-enough.
I am lovable.
I am deserving of love.
I can aspire to great things.
I deserve to be treated fairly.
I deserve to have a loving girlfriend.
I deserve to have a good job.

HOW I WILL MAKE THEM COME TRUE

I will choose people and situations that are good for me.
I will surround myself with people who treat me fairly.
I will read books on assertiveness and practice it in my everyday life.
I will see myself through my own eyes as the good person I am.
I will recognize my abilities and try my best at everything I do.
I will learn to overcome my fear of winning.
I will learn how to receive praise.
I will look for a good job that pays well, and a boss who treats me fairly.
I will allow myself to play my best in sports.
I will look to myself for support.
I will get rid of all people and situations that are hurting me.
I will dream.

Thanks to these Programs, Greg has moved into his own apartment with a recovering alcoholic friend from AA. He is actively looking for another job with better working conditions, and is apprenticing with a woodworker to learn the art of fine furniture repair. He is paying off debts so he can eventually become self-employed, and has had an appreciative, supportive girlfriend for two months.

Your Programs

It's time now to take all the information you've learned so far, and figure out what's been controlling your life. Write your Father's Programs, your Mother's Programs, your Siblings' Programs, and any other Programs from important people in your childhood. Next, write how you obeyed these "commands." It's very important to know your part in saying "yes" to these Programs, to discover how you are responsible for making them true. If you realize your responsibility in this, you'll also see your power to grow and change.

Now, take some time to review your Programs. Are they true? Do you like them? Are you ready to delete them up, to write New Self Programs, to begin anew? It's time to take control of your future, of yourself. Now. Write your own New Self Programs and the ways in which you will make them come true. *Read them daily.* Believe them. Practice them. Make them a part of yourself.

FATHER'S PROGRAMS

_____

_____

_____

_____

_____

_____

_____

_____

_____

_____

_____

_____

_____

_____

HOW I MAKE THEM COME TRUE

_____

_____

_____

_____

_____

_____

_____

_____

_____

_____

_____

_____

_____

MOTHER'S PROGRAMS

_____

_____

_____

_____

_____

_____

_____

_____

_____

_____

_____

_____

_____

HOW I MAKE THEM COME TRUE

_____

_____

_____

_____

_____

_____

_____

_____

_____

_____

_____

_____

_____

SIBLINGS' PROGRAMS

_____

_____

_____

_____

_____

_____

_____

_____

_____

_____

_____

_____

_____

HOW I MAKE THEM COME TRUE

_____

_____

_____

_____

_____

_____

_____

_____

_____

_____

_____

_____

IMPORTANT OTHERS' PROGRAMS

_____

_____

_____

_____

_____

_____

_____

_____

_____

_____

_____

_____

_____

HOW I MAKE THEM COME TRUE

_____

_____

_____

_____

_____

_____

_____

_____

_____

_____

_____

_____

_____

MY NEW SELF PROGRAMS

_____

_____

_____

_____

_____

_____

_____

_____

_____

_____

_____

_____

_____

HOW I WILL MAKE THEM COME TRUE

Homework 1

Once Upon A Time...

Now that you have a clearer idea of your true self, I want you to write your life story. Begin with *"Once upon a time..."* Tell where you were born, what your parents or caretakers were like. Describe your home, your school, your friends. Write your story, your autobiography. Use more paper if you need it, and attach it to this Workbook.

_____

_____

_____

_____

_____

_____

_____

_____

_____

_____

_____

_____

_____

_____

_____

_____

_____

_____

_____

_____

_____

_____

_____

_____

_____

_____

_____

_____

_____

_____

_____

_____

_____

_____

_____

_____

_____

Insights

_____

_____

_____

_____

_____

_____

_____

_____

_____

_____

_____

_____

"The parent who could see his boy as he really is, would shake his head and say " Willie is no good; I'll sell him."

Stephen Butler Leacock, from "Essays and Literary Studies" 1916

Chapter 2

The Search for Bugs

When we return to the **Scene of the Crime**, the Parental Programs become clear. The repeated messages which are given verbally and behaviorally, blatantly and subtly, teach the child who he is, what he is worth, and if he deserves to be loved. As an adult looking back into childhood, we are more rational. We can safely remember; we can feel the hurt and disappointment from a distance. *And we can also choose to believe or not to believe...*

So you've gotten this far, and you're now wondering, *"Is there any hope for me?"* Don't be ridiculous, of course there's hope. Would I write a book just to point out how trapped you are by your Parental Programs without giving you a way out? First, you need to have a *complete mental work-up*. Just like a physical check-up, you have to know what's healthy and what's not. Let's look at your life.

Positive & Negative, Observed, & Circumstantial Programs

Programs are directly installed into your psyche with words and behaviors. I call these **Positive and Negative Programs.** There are also more subtle Programs which are installed by *observing* behaviors or situations. I call these **Observed Programs.** And then there are the Programs given by chance, by fate and situations beyond anyone's control. I call these **Circumstantial Programs.** Look at the following examples.

Negative Programs

Words and actions can give Negative Programs to children.

* Beatings or other physical abuse

* Telling a child he is stupid, ugly, fat, etc.

* Ignoring a child

* Screaming, yelling, swearing

* Telling a child she is unlovable

* Telling a child he is a failure

* Mocking a child's dreams

* Withholding necessities

* Disappointing by not following through on promises

* Allowing the child to be abused by another

* Sexually abusing a child

* Name-calling

* Severe punishment

Negative Observed Programs

Some Programs are learned by watching parental behavior.

* Beating or abusing a spouse or other children

* Constantly quarreling with friends, neighbors, or strangers

* Abusing alcohol or drugs

* Ignoring family responsibilities

* Having difficulty holding a job, or refusing to work

* Displaying a cynical attitude toward people or life

Negative Circumstantial Programs

Sometimes parents' words and actions are misinterpreted by children.

* Paying too much attention to one child, compared to others

* Being away from home too often

* Death of a parent or significant relative

* Dissolving the family through divorce, separation, or abandonment

* Suffering from a serious or long-term illness

* Not spending enough time with a child because of other commitments

Negative Programs

There are three main categories of Negative Programs: **Bad, Worthless, and Unwanted.**
There are many variations of these words and feelings.

You are Bad...

stupid
worthless
no-good
wrong
unable to do anything right
lazy
mean
a bum
ugly, fat, tall, gawky, gangly

You are Worthless...

not-good-enough
not worth my time
constantly in the way
not special
abusable
invisible
stupid
an albatross
silly
weak, spineless
clumsy
pathetic
wrong
a sexual object

You are Unwanted...

invisible
not special
second-rate
insubstantial, unimportant

Manifestations of Negative Programs

Depression
Anxiety
Self-sabotage
Anger
Fear
Addiction
Escapism
Perfectionism
Under Achieving
Over-Achieving
Hopelessness
Unhealthy Relationships

Negative Programs In Disguise

You are perfect
You are so gorgeous.
You will never let me down.
You take care of everything.
I love you more than anyone else ever could.

Manifestations of Negative Programs in Disguise

Anxiety
Perfectionism
Rigidity
Fear
Withdrawal
Over-functioning
Vanity
Over-Achieving
Depression

Positive Programs

You are good.
You are lovable.
You are wonderful.
You are special.
You are wanted.
You are worthy of good things.
You are deserving.
You are attractive.
You are worthwhile.
You are important.
You are kind.
You are good-enough.

Manifestations Of Positive Programs

good self-esteem
healthy relationships
successful in work
happiness
confidence
handle problems well
responsible
adaptable
sociable
moderation in all things
positive attitude in general
trust

Keeping the **Positive & Negative, Observed, and Circumstantial Programs** in mind, let yourself discover your own Programs as you read the following stories. They are good examples of the unconscious power of Negative Programs.

Susan's Story

Susan was a cute little curly-haired two year old when her mother gave her up for adoption. Her adopted parents cared for her as best they knew how, but they often neglected and mistreated her. Not all people who adopt are Ozzie and Harriet. All her life, Susan felt unwanted and not-good-enough. She felt thrown away by her mother, and criticized and judged by her adoptive parents. This self-concept permeated her entire life, and she was very unhappy and lonely much of the time.

Susan's Parental Programs:

"You are unwanted."
"You are not worth our time."
"You are wrong and stupid."
"You are not lovable."

No wonder Susan felt so sad. She made her Programs true in every area of her life. She fell in love with Don Juans who used her and then threw her away. She often "rescued" men who made her feel needed. Men with no money, no jobs, and nothing to offer her.

Rescuing others will inevitably lead you to need rescuing yourself.

At the time of our first session, Susan was seeing a man who told her at the very beginning of their relationship that he could never marry her because she was not of his culture. His Indian family still believed in arranged marriages, and he planned to follow their traditional rituals. It's as if her radar for fulfilling her programming *caused* the attraction. She felt unwanted by him immediately, but still pursued him. He kept her a secret from his family, so she felt unworthy. He couldn't marry her, so she felt unwanted. He often criticized her, so she felt wrong and stupid. He was a perfect match for making her Negative Parental Programs come true.

After a few sessions, she was able to identify her Programs. She was horrified when she looked back on all her relationships and saw the same pattern. She had been quite good at this. But she wanted to stop herself from repeating this craziness in the future. How? First, she wrote her new identity.

New Self Programs:

"I am lovable."
"I am important to everyone in my life."
"I am wanted."
"I am smart, capable, and have good judgment."
"I am special."
"I am a quality person"

The way to implement new Self Programs is to "act as if" you already believe they are true.

If you wait until you *feel* your new Self Programs, you'll be old and gray. So Susan didn't wait. She "acted as if" she already was the new woman she wanted to be. To accomplish this, at every encounter, she asked herself questions.

As a new woman with my New Self Programs...

"Is this person someone a woman with Positive Self Programs would allow into her life?"
"Does this man meet the criteria for a healthy and loving relationship?"
"Is this the kind of man who is capable of loving me as I deserve to be loved?"
"Is this person capable of being a good friend?"

"Is this situation good for me in my new identity as a deserving, quality woman?"

"Does this job make me feel smart, appreciated, and capable?"

"Do my bosses and co-workers treat me with the respect and courtesy I deserve?"

"Am I teaching everyone in my life how I deserve to be treated?"

"Are there areas in my life where I can improve the way I feel?"

"Do I need to weed out certain 'friends' and 'boyfriends' who don't treat me well?"

Susan lives her life *as if* she believes she deserves her new Positive Self Programs.

Screening allows us to shield ourselves from pain and mistreatment.

It's been very hard at times for her to screen out the men who would fulfill her old Negative Programs. She still feels very attracted to them. Old Programs don't die overnight. But by "acting as if," she protects herself from repeating past mistakes, and learns who she really is.

Screening out the "bad" gets rid of drama and chaos, and letting in the "good" ensures peace and love. "Acting as if" has given Susan new experiences which are teaching her she is truly lovable and deserving of attention and respect.

Martha's Story

Martha used comedy to hide the pain she carried inside. Her humor when talking about her brother's teasing and her father's ridicule masked a lifelong depression.

In our first session, Martha told me she was depressed because she hated her job as a secretary.

"I hate my life. I hate being a secretary. But that's all I've ever been, that's all I know. I enrolled in acupuncture school, but felt too guilty to go. Who do I think I am? I'm not smart enough to do that. And I have no social life. I'm dating a man who doesn't really care about me. I met him in my spiritual group. He's driving me crazy. At first we were just friends. He was always very nice to me. I really was attracted to him, and one day he kissed me. I was surprised, but very happy.

He asked me to go away for the weekend with him. We went camping and slept in the same tent, but he didn't come near me. I felt so unwanted, so unattractive. But I didn't say anything. I didn't know what to say, anyway. I don't know what to do. I think we're getting closer, but it feels like something major is missing."

During our first few sessions, I explored Martha's feelings and interpretations regarding the events of her life, both past and present. Going back to her childhood, I learned that Martha's mother was very passive and depressed.

"My mother was just 'there,' if you know what I mean. Mostly, she was out of it. She had a couple of nervous breakdowns and was in and out of the hospital a lot. So she didn't really raise me. My father was rather effeminate but criticized me and my mother for being too feminine. My parents had separate beds for as long as I can remember, and I often overheard their arguments about sex. My father apparently never wanted sex and said my mother was unattractive and unappealing to him. He often brought younger men to the house for dinner. I always thought that was strange. I always wondered why these younger guys would even want to know my father. It was weird."

Martha also had a brother who terrorized her as a child. She describes him as being slow, "not-right," and mean.

"He used to beat me and tease me when we were children. Actually, he did it until I left home at age twenty. He would beat me and tell me I was stupid and ugly. Those words still ring in my head. I hated him. I still do. He's sick. And my mother was too sick herself to stop him, and my father didn't care."

Early on, Martha learned she wasn't very important in her parents' eyes, because her brother was allowed to beat her. When she cried to her mother, she was told to stay out of his way. Because she was often criticized for her appearance, she learned how to be invisible.

Although Martha was an honor roll student in high school, her father told her he wouldn't send her to college because *"you're just a girl and you'll get married and become a secretary."* Her mother often told her she would never marry because men don't like her.

Martha eventually moved out of her parents' house and became a secretary for the next sixteen years, hating each job more than the last. She had a series of unsuccessful relationships with married men.

Martha's Parental Programs

Martha's story is a perfect example of the power of Programs. It was as if her father installed *"married secretary"* in her emotional computer Program. And her mother deleted *"married."* So Martha was left with commands telling her to be an *"unmarried secretary"*.

It was at this point in therapy that I introduced the concept of Parental Programs. Martha was moved as I explained this to her. After several speechless moments, she finally understood her life. The Program metaphor enabled her to look back on the choices she'd made to see how her unconscious need to "follow orders" kept her choices in line with her Programs.

Martha came to the next session very excited. She had spent many hours thinking about her life and the orders to be an unmarried secretary. She'd always felt like a failure, as if she were stupid and unattractive. But now her self-blame and self-doubt dropped away. Knowing the Programs existed, she now understood why she'd felt so guilty when she enrolled in acupuncture school: *She was going against her Programs.*

Martha was curious about how she had remained unmarried, even though she consciously believed she wanted to marry. In our exploration of her past relationships with men, we saw she dated only married and gay men. She'd made the *"unmarried"* part of her Program come true by choosing *only* men who would never be interested in marrying her: gay men and married men. She followed her Programs perfectly!

There came a time in therapy when she was able to analyze her father's behavior and attitude toward women, and was able to admit to herself that he was probably secretly gay. His resentment toward her mother's and her sexuality, his hostility, blaming behavior and criticism toward anything feminine seemed to point to that conclusion. This was almost confirmed in Martha's mind when she painfully learned her present boyfriend was gay. Freud's theory of repetition compulsion, our tendency to repeat the past, was remarkably illustrated here. It was extremely synchronistic when all of this occurred during this critical time in Martha's therapy.

Empathic understanding of her pain in dealing with these discoveries was extremely important. She was re-experiencing her father's rejection of her as a feminine being. And during this time, as I sat with her and gave her support, our relationship became stronger on a deeper level. It felt to me as if she experienced this as something we were going through together. The support she felt gave her the strength to face the truth about her boyfriend, and more importantly, about her father.

It was also during this time that she started to wear makeup and more feminine clothing. She became consciously aware of this change when she bought a pink sweater.

"I realized my father would have ridiculed me if I'd worn such a feminine piece of clothing. I feel free to wear whatever I want to wear now. He can't stop me anymore. I can be feminine without fearing his criticism. I never realized how his influence was still in my life."

There was a lightness about her as she said this, an affect of peaceful self-acceptance. Now, it was also important for her to see her Sibling's Programs. Her brother had told her she was stupid and ugly, and she had quasi-obeyed that Program by *feeling* stupid and ugly. In truth, she was exceptionally bright and gifted, and quite pretty. She had learned to disguise her intelligence by hiding behind a job that offered her no personal satisfaction. And she disguised her beauty by wearing unfeminine clothing and no make-up.

This story has a happy ending. When Martha understood herself in terms of her Parental Programs for *"unmarried secretary,"* she became free to write her own Programs. She visualized herself deleting her Parental and Sibling Programs and saw herself typing in *"inner happiness, good relationship with a man, wonderful job."* She eventually quit her secretarial job, moved to a small town more in tune with her own character, and began a career in a field which brings her satisfaction and inner happiness. She has a new relationship with a co-worker who treats her with kindness, love, and respect.

Daniel's Story

Daniel is a forty year old married man, father of two sons, ages eighteen and nineteen. His wife and boys are currently taking Prozac and are under psychiatric care. They have all been diagnosed as suffering from Major Depression.

Approximately one year ago, when I first met Daniel, no one in his family was in therapy or on medication.

"I am overwhelmed. I can't do this anymore. I am carrying everyone. It's too much for me. I can't take care of them anymore. I feel like running away."

Daniel had been taking care of everyone in his family. He was acting as father, mother, rescuer, caretaker, teacher, doctor, and therapist. No one else was functioning. He loved his wife and two sons, and believed that he had done everything he could do to help them. But no one was helping him.

Daniel's parents were divorced shortly after his mother abandoned the family when he was five. His father, a military man, remarried shortly thereafter, and was absent most of the next several years, leaving Daniel and his younger brother under the care of the step-mother. Daniel was sexually abused by her from the ages of eight through thirteen.

Daniel wrote the following:

"During these years, my step-mother abused me psychologically, emotionally, physically, and sexually. We were two good little boys wanting and needing a real mommy who loved us back. Instead, she treated us as if we were monsters, who needed to be beaten and raped into submission to be adequately controlled. It became normal to be beaten up by her. Sometimes she beat me so hard, I would get knocked out from punches to the face and head. When I regained consciousness, it was not uncommon to find that I was lying on the floor while she was still kicking me. In that twilight just before full consciousness, I would often say to myself, 'She is still hurting me. Why is she doing this? Am I a bad boy? I do not remember doing anything bad.' As time passed, we believed that the beatings occurred for two reasons; because we had done something wrong, and because she liked to beat us. Soon I began to believe that I was bad and no-good and probably born that way. I knew on some level something was wrong with our family, but I didn't know what. I reasoned this because I knew my friends were not being beaten by their parents. So I began to think that maybe I was just born bad and that I deserved this beating. So I never complained to my father. He wasn't around much anyway.

"When I was eleven, my body was beginning to look more like my father's. My step-mother had already turned our relationship into a sexual one by my eigth birthday. Now, at night when my brother was asleep, she would come into our room and lie in my bed. Then she would caress me, fondle my penis, and with her fingers, commit sodomy with me. Frightened, I would pretend to be asleep. As sick as it sounds, I was scared, but I also liked her tenderness. It was the closest thing to love I ever felt from her."

Daniel left home to join the service at age seventeen, and has had little interaction with any of his family since that time. He joined a very strict church and became a devoted follower of its rules and beliefs. He married his wife soon after. He describes his marriage as extremely satisfying, despite her depression.

When Daniel began therapy, he was feeling angry that his life was so disrupted by their problems because, in spite of everything, he considered himself to be a happy person by nature. He felt frustrated and powerless to change his situation. His religion forbids divorce, and he still felt very much in love with his wife. He felt his only relief from this burden would be to run away.

Daniel had never received prior therapy and had never dealt with his own issues. During the past year of treatment (twice weekly), Daniel has learned to create boundaries in his life and has discontinued over-functioning for his family members. He stopped "treating" them and reassuring them and taking care of their sadness. When his wife or sons came to him with their depressive feelings and problems, he empathized but offered no solutions. He simply advised them to go to a mental health professional for help. As a result, they were all left to feel their own pain. This gave them the motivation to seek their own treatment with real professionals who could offer real help. With therapy and medical evaluations, it was determined that they suffered from a clinical (chemical) depression, and all were placed on Prozac. Depression often runs in families, and in this case, the sons obviously inherited the depression gene from their mother.

After a few months, the oldest son returned to college and the youngest son started his first job. Daniel's wife feels much relief from the lifting of her own depression which has significantly improved their relationship. She says it feels like a lifelong gray cloud has lifted, and she can see the sunshine for the first time in her life. She has also begun psychotherapy to work on her low self-esteem issues. With the alleviation of surrounding family problems, Daniel has been free to work on his own issues of low self-esteem and underlying depression as a result of the sexual abuse inflicted by his step-mother. He has also worked on his feeling of abandonment which stemmed from his biological mother's leaving at an early age. Daniel feels a greater sense of control in his life and in his dealings with others. At the present time, he is working on his feelings of powerlessness and abandonment which are exhibited in outbursts of anger. He works extremely hard in his therapy, and is highly motivated for growth and change.

There are several Scenes of the Crime in Daniel's life. At age five, his mother left the family. His father was absent while in the service and left him in the care of the evil step-mother. His step-mother physically beat him in the daytime, and sexually abused him in the nighttime.

Mother's Parental Program:

"You are not worthy of my love and presence."

Father's Parental Program:

"You are not worthy of my love and presence."
"You deserve the abuse you are getting."

Step-Mother's Program:

"You are bad, unworthy of love, deserve to be beaten."
"You are a sexual object."
"You are to be used."

These Programs were living at the very core of Daniel's being, and not so easily released. In our work together, Daniel is becoming aware of his faulty beliefs, and has learned how he came to believe these negative ideas about himself.

Victim or Aggressor?

Victims often believe there are only two positions: victim or aggressor. This is why it's so common for a victim to become an aggressor later in life. If you believe that your choices are to be either the victim or the aggressor, it is understandable why one would choose to be the latter. For example, it is likely that a man who beats his children was himself beaten as a child.

You give what you got.

When Daniel experiences frustration, anger, or negativity, he feels he has two choices: to be the victim or the aggressor. In his relationship with his wife, he has been extremely verbally abusive. He exhibits controlling behavior on a regular basis. This fits in with his wife's Parental Programs, since she was raised by a verbally abusive alcoholic father. In times of stress, Daniel's fight or flight response is to become the aggressor so that he doesn't become the victim. In therapy, Daniel is learning that there is another choice. It is **Assertiveness**, a way of becoming what I call *Quietly Powerful*.

The "Quietly Powerful" Rules

10 Rules For A Good Argument

1. **NO swearing.**

   You can feel anger and love at the same time.

2. **NO name-calling.**

   There is no place for meanness in a healthy relationship.

3. **NO interrupting.**

   You will have your turn to speak.

4. **NO screaming.**

   Louder does not make you right.

5. **NO physical threats or acts of violence.**

   It is against the law, against nature, and not nice.

6. **NEVER use the words "NEVER" or "ALWAYS".**

   Use words like "often," "hardly ever," "seldom," "most of the time."

7. **NO threats to end the relationship.**

   Decisions pertaining to ending relationships should be made in calm moments of rational thinking, after much thought and discussion.

8. **NO lying or exaggerating.**

   Don't add to the problem by making it bigger than it is.

9. **NO over-generalizing.**

   Stay with one topic at a time. Be specific.

10. **NO manipulating.**

    It makes you look bad.

Instead... BE QUIETLY POWERFUL

1. Speak in a normal, calm voice.

Respect your partner, even when you are angry. If you yell or lose control, you're giving your partner ammunition to use against you, and making yourself look silly. *What you are saying is very powerful if you quietly speak your truth.*

2. Agree on a time to argue.

Sometimes, you need time to think or to calm down. Ask your partner if now is a good time to talk, or agree on a future time. You have the right to talk or not talk.

3. Listen. Take turns speaking.

Some Native American Indians use a "talking stick." Only the one who holds the stick is allowed to speak. If helpful, try holding a pen or an object in your hand, and pass it to your partner when you are done speaking. Pass it back and forth to avoid interruptions.

4. Stick to one topic.

One argument at a time. If necessary, make a list of the things you would like to straighten out, one issue at a time.

5. Repeat what your partner is telling you to show you hear and understand, even though you may not agree.

"I hear you saying that..." It's called "Active Listening."

6. Acknowledge your part in the conflict.

There are two of you, and chances are, there's been a misunderstanding that needs to be resolved. Look at your own behavior and words, too.

7. Apologize.

Admit your part.
Forgiveness and resolution can't occur until someone says "I'm sorry."

8. Be willing to compromise for resolution.

The most important thing is to reach an agreement where everyone feels heard, loved, and close once again.

As Daniel gains in self-esteem, he feels more confident in behaving in **Quietly Powerful** ways. His relationships are enhanced by this more rational approach, and the outcomes leave him feeling powerful, successful, and lovable. Daniel's therapy will continue to explore his Parental Programs, his childhood injuries, and his present life choices. He will someday fully rewrite his own Programs for self-love and acceptance.

"Recently, I have learned to accept and love myself. It is true that my first sixteen years passed through some very troubled times. Although I feel a sense of loss, I am not angry for missing out on a healthy and strong father-son and mother-son relationship. Step-Mother did evil things to my brother and me. I overcame and transcended her violence and sexual abuse. The important idea here is that those bad experiences were truly as bad as they were, and that I choose to let the good experiences be more powerfully good. I am thankful for those good times with my friends. I am on earth to do better than just survive life. I can help others who have hurts like I had and like I have still. It can be done. I have a fearless determination to take my place among other transcenders of abuse."

Your Turn

Now it's time to look back into your own life. By using the stories as guides, examine your childhood. Remember the little moments, the uneventful days, the small occurrences, and the family rituals. Life is often made up of ordinary events, strung together by plain and simple days. Using *Questionnaire 2: Who Told You That?* to help you remember your childhood-self, go on to do *The "Act As If" Exercise* to practice being your deserving-self. *The "Quietly Powerful" Exercise* will help you find power in your adult-self. *Homework 2: Keep A Journal* will give you a lifetime tool for self-expression, clarity, focus, and a sense of your own history.

Questionnaire 2

Who Told You That?

1. Who are you most like in your family?

_____

_____

_____

_____

2. What relative do you look like? Sound like? Act like?

_____

_____

_____

_____

3. Whose life is most similar to yours?

_____

_____

_____

_____

4. Who told you who you were when you were a child?

_____

_____

_____

_____

5. Whose opinion in your family matters most to you?

_____

_____

_____

_____

6. Do you have a favorite relative? Why?

_____

_____

_____

_____

7. How often do you see your relatives?

_____

_____

_____

_____

8. Are you treated by family members in the same way you were
   treated as a child? Do you take on the same role?

_____

_____

_____

_____

_____

_____

_____

The "Act As If" Exercise

***Purpose: * To teach you how to live by your New Self Programs
before you actually feel deserving of them***

Behave "as if" you already believe your New Self Programs. Do not wait until a miracle happens to make you feel entitled to be the person you were meant to be. Just be who you are. Forget your insecurities, fears, and feelings of unworthiness. "Act as if" you have great love, respect, and admiration for yourself. Make choices "as if" you think and feel you are great and deserving of the best. *Pretend* you believe you deserve the best, in all areas of your life. In love and work. Just do it. It will change your life, and you will grow. Trust me.

The "Quietly Powerful" Exercise

Purpose: * *To find your inner power*
               * *To learn to speak from a centered place of confidence*

Practice being **Quietly Powerful** in your everyday life, especially at home. Home is our most difficult place to function because of the intimacy we experience. It is in our closest relationships where we need to do the most work on ourselves, because it is here where we learn and grow the most. Our family is our best teacher.

There are many wonderful assertiveness training books devoted totally to this subject, and I highly recommend taking the time to study this subject in depth. Becoming **Quietly Powerful** in an assertive way will free you more than any other tool I can offer.

Homework 2

Keep A Journal

One of the easiest ways to measure your growth and change is through keeping a journal. You may think you have nothing to write. It doesn't matter. I want you to express your feelings about your days to yourself. When you become comfortable "talking" to yourself in writing, it often makes it easier to communicate with others. When we think to ourselves, our thoughts, feelings, and ideas come in randomly, often making no sense. In writing, we are required to organize our thinking in a different way. You'll be surprised at what you learn about yourself when you later read what you have written.

I have kept a daily journal since I was eleven years old. I don't often read them, because the reward lies in the act of writing. But when I do, I can see different stages and lessons in my life, and it gives me perspective I never would have known. I use a blank sketching book from an artist's supply shop. I can write one sentence, or five pages per day. I can draw a picture, or write a poem. Whatever I feel like. I like to write at the end of the day when all of my feelings are fresh. You decide when it's best for you.

Just begin today.

Insights

_____

_____

_____

_____

_____

_____

_____

_____

_____

_____

_____

_____

_____

_____

_____

_____

_____

_____

_____

_____

_____

_____

_____

_____

_____

_____

_____

"If only we could know what was going on in a baby's mind while observing him in action we could certainly understand everything there is to psychology."

Jean Piaget, from "La Premiere Annee de l'Enfant" 1927

Chapter 3

Boundaries

Happy people surround themselves with people who are good, kind, honest, funny, supportive, and caring. Unhappy people don't screen and let destructive and draining people into their lives.

If you meet someone at work or have a next-door neighbor, it doesn't mean these people have to be allowed into your life. Unlike our family, we get to choose our friends. The more entitled we feel, the more selective we become. We are not victims of those who want to know us. We can decide. We can develop screens which let in the good and keep out the bad. Without screens, there are no boundaries. Without boundaries, there is chaos.

Monique's Story

When I first met Monique, I was in awe of her ability to speak so eloquently. She was a professional writer, and it showed. If I had written down her words, there would be no need to edit. She came to me after her last therapist had violated her boundaries. This male psychologist had treated her for two years for mild depression due to a lack of success in her journalism career. She adored him, and treated him more like a guru.

"If Dr. G said I should do something, I did it. I believed he knew what was good for me, and I trusted him with my life. Hard to believe, because trust never came easy for me. He would tell me stories of his life, which I thought was a little odd, but I felt like he was sharing a part of him with me that he didn't with other patients. I looked forward to every session, and only now do I realize I wasn't getting the help I needed. It felt like I was there to tell him how great he was as a therapist, and I felt like I should 'get better' for his sake. Then one day, he asked if I would like to have a session in his home. He said it would be beneficial for our relationship. Again, I felt it was odd, but I trusted him, obviously more than I trusted myself. Well, one thing led to another and he came on to me. I was devastated and ran to my car in tears. I still don't know how I got home."

This is a classic case of boundary violation between patient and therapist.

Psychotherapy never includes socializing or sex.

Monique was betrayed by her doctor. And betrayal and loss feel terribly familiar to her. Let's look at her **Scene of the Crime.**

When she was four, her parents left her with a senile aunt while her little sister was being born. She remembered this nightmarish time with horror, and described her aunt as the Wicked Witch of the West. When she was allowed to return to her parents two weeks later, she found her mother's attention was totally taken by the baby. Monique felt abandoned and betrayed. Life had been lovely until her brother was born, and now it felt like the party was over. Also there were lots of beatings as she grew up, but she usually felt unaware of what she had done wrong. There didn't seem to be a system of logic in place, and so she was left to guess how to be good. At age ten, her father was transferred out of state, and so she lost all of her friends. Two years later, her parents divorced. It felt to her that "having" meant "losing". She had lost her special bond with her mother when her brother was born, she had lost her friends at school when she moved, and she had lost her father after the divorce.

Life's Programs:

"Having is temporary."
"Having is losing."
"Loss is inevitable."
"Nothing is safe."

And then she lost her psychologist after his betrayal. When she came to see me, she had many of the symptoms of Post Traumatic Stress Disorder, even though she hadn't been exposed to a physically life-threating event. Her emotional integrity had been threatened which resulted in many of the same symptoms.

Symptoms of Post Traumatic Stress Disorder

* **Intense fear, helplessness, or horror**
* **Recurrent, intrusive, distressing recollections of the event**
* **Recurrent dreams of the event**
* **A sense of reliving the event, illusions, hallucinations**
* **Intense stress at events that resemble the event**
* **Physical reactions on exposure to events that resemble the occurrence**
* **Avoidance of thoughts, feelings, or conversations about the event**
* **Inability to recall all of the event**
* **Feelings of detachment, alienation from others**
* **Lack of interest in normal activities**
* **Inability to make future plans**
* **Sleep disturbance**
* **Irritability**
* **Lack of concentration**
* **Hypervigilance**
* **Significant distress which impairs normal life functioning**

In our work together, it was important for Monique to learn to trust me as her psychologist. I explained to her that I would not be telling her stories about myself. I disclose very little to my patients about my personal life. It is inappropriate and it gets in the way of the work. This is a boundary. I also explained to her that I would never see her outside of my office. This boundary enables a patient to feel safe enough to tell me anything. I will not be at her next party, and we will not be having coffee. Monique learned that she could be whoever she wanted to be in my office. I did not expect her to be "the perfect patient," whatever she thought that to be. I did expect her to be on time for her appointments, and to regard our weekly time as something she could count on. These boundaries made it safe for her to explore herself and to let the session time be hers.

At first, Monique felt a little uncomfortable having all the focus on her. With time, she learned to trust the boundaries, and therefore, me. We worked on her need to develop a screen to make her own boundaries. It was hard for her at first, but later she learned to trust her inner wisdom. It was there all the time, like when she felt uncomfortable with her previous psychologist. Had she listened to her wise voice within, she would have terminated therapy with him long before the sexual boundary violation occurred.

And because she developed boundaries, she also felt entitlement for the first time in her life. She became righteously angry and reported the psychologist to the Board of Psychology, and also filed a civil suit against him. It gave her great satisfaction to stand up for her self, and to enforce her boundaries.

Monique's New Self Programs:

"Having is keeping."
"I am deserving of love and attention."
"I can decide the boundaries in all of my relationships."

David's Story

When I first met David, he had no job and no relationships. Referred for therapy by the Office of Vocational Rehabilitation, a state agency that works with people disabled by physical or emotional problems, he was looking to create a life for himself. He had suffered from Major Depression during the past year, after the death of his only brother.

David had been sexually molested by his mother until he was eleven years old. Not only did he suffer the usual feelings of guilt, shame, self-hatred, and despair, but the manner of her abuse complicated it even further. The sexual encounters consisted of her touching him, while he was required to stay very still. He was not allowed to touch her, nor was he allowed to initiate. Her mixed message was, *"Come here, go away."*

David's Mother's Programs:

"You are the passive one."
"You cannot initiate."
"You are a sexual object."
"You are not deserving of protection."
"You are not allowed to be a simple little boy."

David's way of making his Programs true was easy. *Don't initiate. Be passive.* This does not make for a very satisfying life. Not only was he unable to go after the education or work that he preferred, he was also incapable of initiating relationships with women. He was, therefore, left alone with no meaningful work. The Major Depression was a natural outcome of years of **"wanting, not having."**
After David identified his Programs, he decided it was time to take the risk to grow and change.

David's New Self Programs:

"I can be cause, not just effect."
"I can initiate."
"I can go after the education and work that I prefer."
"I can go after women I am attracted to and ask them out."
"I can decide to make new beginnings."
"I can pursue whatever and whomever I want."

The first thing David did was to tell the Vocational Rehabilitation counselor that he was interested in computers. He had silently waited for them to "discover" this in his career aptitude test results. No longer willing to wait for people to guess correctly or to read his mind, he made his preferences known everywhere. He felt freer to initiate conversations with strangers in grocery stores, and learned that nothing bad happened. He learned he could initiate in all areas of his life, and most of the time, he had good results. This was totally unlike the experiences he had had with his mother during the sexual abuse. He even got up the courage to ask a woman for coffee. She sat next to him in his computer class, and her friendliness made it easier. Still, in the past, he would have waited for her to ask him.

David is well on his way to a new life, one that *he* chooses, with a sense of deservingness and self-love.

Your Turn

In looking at your ability now to have boundaries and to have a clearly defined sense of yourself, answer *Questionnaire 3A: Who Do You Think You Are?* and *Questionnaire 3B: Jealousy or Possessiveness?* It will help you learn more about yourself to prepare you for *The "Island" Exercise*. Knowing who you are helps to center you in everyday life. It empowers you to say "yes" to the good and "no" to the bad that comes into your life's path. *Homework 3: House Cleaning* will assist you in your search for clarity.

Questionnaire 3A

Who Do You Think You Are?

1. When you were younger, how were you different than you are today?

_____

_____

_____

_____

2. Have you ever thought differently about yourself?

_____

_____

_____

_____

3. Do you like yourself? Do you like how you look?

_____

_____

_____

_____

4. What would you change about your personality?

_____

_____

_____

_____

5. What prevents you from making this change?

_____

_____

_____

6. How would you describe your relationships?

_____

_____

_____

_____

7. Who do you admire most? Who would you wish to be more like?

_____

_____

_____

_____

8. What traits do you admire in others?

_____

_____

_____

_____

_____

_____

_____

_____

_____

Questionnaire 3B

Jealousy Or Possessiveness?

1. You're at a party and you see your date/spouse talking to a very attractive person of the opposite sex. What do you do?

   a. Glare at them from across the room, hoping you'll scare them into ending the conversation.
   b. Join them, letting the other person know that he/she "belongs" to you.
   c. Look the other way.
   d. Let them be. Find an interesting person to talk to, knowing that it's natural and normal for both of you to have platonic conversations and relationships.

2. You find tell-tale signs of infidelity. What do you do?

   a. Confront and accuse your mate with the cheating evidence, watch him/her squirm, and throw him/her out.
   b. Leave suspicious phone numbers lying around.
   c. Look the other way. This will go away.
   d. Share your thoughts and fears with your mate and discuss the situation calmly.

3. Your spouse tells you that he has had an affair. It's over, and will never happen again. What do you do?

   a. End the relationship immediately. There is no trust left.
   b. Have an affair with his friend.
   c. Forgive and forget. It happens to everyone.
   d. Realize the affair is a symptom of a greater problem in the marriage, and seek counseling.

4. Every time your mate goes out with friends, you are certain that he/she is having an affair. What should you do?

   a. Spy on him/her to catch them in the act.
   b. Ask a lot of questions when he/she returns. Look for slip-ups.
   c. What you don't know won't hurt you.
   d. If you have no real reason to have these fears, consult a professional to learn about your own insecurities.

5. Your mate is excessively flirtatious with one of your attractive friends. You trust that nothing will happen, but you still feel jealous. What should you do?

    a. Tell your mate to stop embarrassing you in front of your friend.
    b. Flirt with his/her best friend.
    c. Be safe and keep your friend away.
    d. Calmly discuss your mate's behavior and try to understand the attraction. Find out if this is an innocent flirtation or a need for more attention.

Results

The responses are designed to show your tendency towards normal jealous reactions or neurotic possessive overreacting.

    A. Aggressive
    B. Revengeful
    C. Passive, in denial
    D. Healthy jealousy

The "Island" Exercise

Purpose: ** To discover your true identity,*
            beyond your roles and possessions

Focus on yourself.

I say these three words constantly when working with men and women in unhappy relationships. They come in saying, *"He said this...She did that...Do you think he loves me?...Will she want me?..."* And my response is always the same. *"What do you want?...What do you feel?...What are your needs?...Does this relationship make you happy?"* When in a relationship, it appears to be human nature to become focused on the other person. We are often more in touch with their desires, feelings, beliefs, opinions, and preferences than with our own. We try to please, we try to capture their love and attention. So focused are we on them, we lose ourselves. We make them our "gods," our reason for being. We become less important to ourselves. Our needs and feelings and desires become unfocused and we lose part of our identity. We become a "we" first and an "I" second. Always a mistake. Our sense of individuality and separateness must remain constant, must remain intact if the relationship is to be healthy. We must be two distinct, healthy, separate individuals who come together to enrich each other's lives. The alternative is two incomplete misfits who feel they need each other to stand up and be acceptable. A relationship based on unhealthy need is always disastrous.

We sometimes begin a relationship feeling relatively whole. We may have been in a process of self-discovery and growth, perhaps in therapy, a 12-Step Program, or spiritual development on some level. We've learned that we most often find relationships when we aren't looking. So we pretend we aren't looking while we secretly look. So there we are, pursuing our hobbies and interests, having been told that we will meet someone special by actively doing the things we enjoy. And then it happens. We meet "special" and we're off. *And this is where most of our childhood "stuff" comes out in really weird ways.* This is where the de-focusing on self begins. Almost immediately. We accommodate, adjust, adapt so that we can "make this work." Accommodating, adjusting, and adapting are very wonderful adjectives if applied to someone who is aware and focused on *self* at the same time.

Focusing on the other in order to please, in order to keep the love we think we need, creates a loss of the self, a lessening of identity. A repressed self, a missing self, can only result in depression, anger, and resentment. We know this already, because most of us have done this before.

So what do we do instead? How do we focus on ourselves, know who we are on a deeper level, and remain an "I" in the context of a "We"?

I Am An Island

I have developed an exercise that seems to put people back in touch with their deepest core identity. Our core identity is the "I" in relation to no one. Not the "I" as someone's mother, father, lover, wife, husband, employer, friend, or child. Not the relational "I." Just "I."

Close your eyes and gently let your mind flow with the following exercise. If you'd like, read it slowly into a tape recorder and play it back for yourself, or have someone read it to you.

The Island Exercise

Imagine you are on a beautiful, peaceful, safe tropical island. The sun is shining and the temperature is perfect. What does it look like? What are the sights, the sounds., the smells ......Take time to feel it.

Breathe deeply and relax. Now, I want you to imagine you are shipwrecked and alone on this island. And no one is ever going to come. You will live on this island by yourself for the rest of your life. What do you do? How do you live? How do you spend your days? How do you make your life meaningful, productive, happy? Are you able to live an enriched life? What are your feelings? Do they change? Do you enjoy the process of finding and preparing food? Do you create art and clothes from palm leaves? Do you take long, exploratory walks, make friends with the animals? Do you wear clothes, swim naked in the ocean? Do you sit quietly, meditate, cry in despair? Are you overwhelmed with the responsibility of total care for all of your needs? Do you run on the beach, or grow fat and lazy? Do you decorate your body with shells and seaweed, or do you simply not care about your appearance? Who are you? Do you like this fantasy, or does it terrify you? Continue to imagine yourself on this island. Feel the sun on your skin, hear the ocean waves and the cries of the seagulls. Feel the sand on your feet and the wind in your hair. See the blue sky and turquoise waters. Feel the life inside of you. Feel your sense of self. Just you.

Some people respond with fear, dread, and total depression at the thought of living alone for the rest of their lives. Others look within and find joy in the discovery of themselves. This is an extreme case of focusing on the Self. There is no "other" to provide a sense of wholeness and completion to the "I." There is just "I." And although "no man is an island," we are ultimately alone, whether we're on a deserted island or in a marriage with six children. The healthiest of us can cultivate our own souls, water ourselves with love, give ourselves what we need for our own sense of harmony and happiness. Self-reliance creates self-love.

We are healthiest when we no longer need our relationships but instead freely choose them.

Our sense of aloneness is not experienced as loneliness, as something to be feared. Our aloneness is our core knowledge of "I," free to connect in givingness and lovingness.

Do this Exercise whenever you're feeling lonely, dependent, needy, or vulnerable. It will put you back in touch with your true self; your highest, wisest, strongest self.

Marlena's Story

Let's look at how Marlena used *The "Island Exercise"* to help free herself from her addiction to a horrible relationship. Marlena is a perfect example of a woman who has no clear sense of self unless she's with a man. She could only define herself in relation to other people; she called herself a forty-six year old mother of two grown children, a daughter, and Bobby's girlfriend. She could have said she was a physical therapist, a sculptor, and a runner. All true, but those self-identities didn't seem to matter in her eyes. And so Marlena came to therapy because she couldn't tolerate her feelings of sadness and hopelessness any longer.

"I'm so miserable I could scream. I'm in love with a man who is so wonderful and loving and kind, who takes care of me, loves me, and really knows how to make me feel good about myself. Because he's afraid of intimacy, he has another woman in his life to make him feel safer, and I can understand that. I'm here to help him break through his fears so he can be with just me."

Marlena had a problem. Her boyfriend had a girlfriend.

Do you know how often women come into my office with psychological evaluations of their boyfriends? They sound like clinical casebooks, describing these men with pop-psychology terms, making themselves feel like they have some control over their situation. Can you imagine "Thelma and Louise" with insight?

Thelma: *"Yeah, my poor husband Darryl came from a family where the men weren't allowed to express their feelings. I know he loves me, and if he'd only go into therapy to meet his inner child, I just know he would be able to give me the love I need."*

Louise: *"Yeah, Thel, I know what you mean. My boyfriend, Jimmy, he just can't let go of the outer macho mask that completely protects him from being hurt. His last girlfriend left him, and his fear of abandonment has left him with a fear of commitment."*

Favorite sister

If we look into Marlena's childhood, if we go to the Scene of the Crime, we learn how and why she would tolerate this scenario.

Marlena is the younger of two girls. She always felt her sister received more attention, more praise, more understanding, and more love than she did. She has countless childhood examples of why this is true. She even has stories of favoritism towards her sister today. And when I hear them, I can readily agree with her. Her mother *does* give her sister more things, more understanding, more time, more everything. And my guess is that it's because her sister is less smart, less pretty, less capable, less successful, less everything. It's ironic that Marlena's "more-than" quality when compared with her sister has caused her pain. As a little girl, and as an adult, she never once thought, *"My sister is not as capable as I am, and therefore needs more from my mother."* Instead, she forgot or never knew and appreciated herself for who she truly is. What many parents never really "get" is that children can't see themselves by themselves. If they are all things good, they still need their parents to *tell* them they are good.

Children Need Mirrors

We all need other people to reflect back an image of ourselves. It's why we say *"Look at what I've done!"* even as adults. Children especially need mirrors. Marlena's "mirrors" took it for granted that she knew how wonderful she was, and instead mirrored her "not as capable" sister. And so, Marlena received a Parental Program: *You are second-best.*

And so she competes. With the girlfriend. For time and attention. And she believes him when he tells her he loves her, that he has a hard time with commitment, and he's only with the other woman because he feels sorry for her, that it's only a matter of time before they can be together. A typical "married man" scenario.

She takes the pain, humiliation, abuse, and crumbs he offers because she believes this is all she deserves. After all, it's been programmed for her that she's second-best. She doesn't feel worthy to have *all* the attention, to be the only one, to be loved and wanted completely in a monogamous relationship. She has a litany of sad love stories. And this is her identity.

How Marlena Makes Her Programs Come True:

"I am second-best. And I do it well. I hang in there. I have hope. I let myself believe that Bobby really wants only me, but he has to be there with her because he feels sorry for her."
"I don't feel I deserve to be the most important one, the number one priority. I accept this."
"I am not good enough to be the only one, so I'm with a married man."

Marlena and I worked on her self-esteem and her feelings of inadequacy. But it wasn't until we discovered her Parental Programs that she was finally able to let go. She realized she had always felt second-best, and was no longer willing to live in that role. It was time to be Number One.
She broke up with him, as she had done fifty times before. But even he sensed that somehow this time was different.

"I told him I was no longer willing to be in second place. I made no demands. I actually said very little. It had all been said before. I just said I wasn't going to play this game anymore. I felt like I was taking my precious marbles home, to give them to someone more deserving in the future."

When Marlena did **The "Island" Exercise**, she was initially very depressed and visualized a bleak, remote, desert island with little vegetation, no animals, and lots of rain. As her sense of self returned and her focus turned inward, she was able to touch her true core self. Her island became lush with life, warmth, and a sense of peace. As we worked in therapy and her self-esteem improved, she wasn't willing to put up with the second-best role, and required first-place attention from the men in her life. When she repeated **The "Island" Exercise**, she found she was able to find happiness on the island by herself.

Today, Marlena is dating. She still feels an initial attraction towards the unavailable charming men, drawn by their sexuality and wit. But she also sees through their outer masks rather quickly, *like every woman can when she chooses to be awake to reality*. And knowing her Parental Programs, she has deleted them and has rewritten her own.

"I am lovable. "
"I am first. "
"I am special."

Homework 3

House Cleaning

Now that you've taken inventory of yourself and your lifestyle, it's time to make your relationships and surroundings reflect your true self. Make your appearance, your home, your possessions, and your family and friends an outer expression of your inner self. It's time to clean out closets, **getting rid of everything that isn't you**. It's time to put your belongings in order, and to clean away clutter that reflects old cluttered Programs. It's time to lose the weight that is no longer you. And, it's also time to clean away people that are negative and draining of your positive energy. Clear away everything and everyone in your life that doesn't add to your life. **This is about establishing boundaries.** Take an inventory of your friends. Are they good, kind, honest, funny, supportive, and caring? Or are they draining of your time and energy? Are they your equals, or do you rescue strays? Look at your mate. Ask yourself the same questions. Have you chosen someone who reflects your true self and your needs? Or are you a caretaker? Remember, this is about being self-ful, not self-ish. And in the future, when new people and situations want to come into your life, remember to be aware of your boundaries. Screen. Is this person good, kind, honest; an equal? Is this situation one that will enhance your life? Be careful what you let enter into your inner life. You'll have to live with the consequences. Screening makes all the difference in the world.

Insights

_____

_____

_____

_____

_____

_____

_____

_____

_____

_____

_____

_____

"If there is anything that we wish to change in the child, we should first examine it and see whether it is not something that could better be changed in ourselves."

C.G. Jung, from "The Integration of the Personality" 1939

Chapter 4

Emotional & Physical Crashes

The Mindbody Connection is very strong, as researched by medical doctors like Bernie Siegel and Larry Dossey. According to Deepak Chopra, M.D., when we're happy, our bodies make "happy chemicals". Our immune systems are strengthened. When we're unhappy, our bodies make "unhappy chemicals". Our immune systems are weakened. We're electro-magnetic-chemical human beings. We are biological organisms with intellectual, emotional, and spiritual components. And all of these elements interplay at all times.

Sometimes, we have physical illnesses and symptoms caused purely by emotional stress. We call this "psychosomatic". The following stories illustrate this phenomenon.

Helen's Story

Helen is a very feminine and gentle twenty-six year old woman who reminded me of a Breck girl. She had an angelic quality that made her appear serene and calm. But her outer tranquillity disguised her inner turmoil. She had been experiencing panic attacks for the past six months.

She first sought medical help, hoping it was a physical condition that could be cured with a pill. After extensive and expensive medical testing, she was found to be the picture of health. She was then referred to me by her HMO's Primary Care Physician to find the underlying psychological cause.

"My body trembled. My heart pounded in my chest. I was sweating all over. 'My God, please don't let me die. Don't let me have an aneurysm' was all I could think. I looked around the office. Everyone else seemed to be working diligently, not noticing the terror that was encompassing my body. I needed desperately to get out of there. I walked to the window, biting my nails and consciously jerking myself along the way, hoping it would return my body back to normal. At the window, I glanced down at the busy city streets seventeen floors below, trying to get my mind on something other than dying. It didn't work."

What Helen described is a classic panic attack, one of the many symptoms of the imprisoning disease of **agoraphobia**.

Symptoms of panic attack:

* **Palpitations, irregular heartbeat**
* **Chest pain, pressure**
* **Difficulty breathing, shortness of breath**
* **Dizziness**
* **Trembling**
* **Sweating**
* **Inability to concentrate**
* **Generalized anxiety**
* **Faintness**
* **Fear of vomiting**
* **Fear of dying**
* **Fear of going insane**
* **Fear of losing control**

These feelings came upon her suddenly, without warning, without apparent reason. One of the reasons the panic attack is so frightening is because *there is no warning or obvious cause.* If we're in a situation of impending danger, these feelings of panic are very normal responses. They are part of biology's "fight or flight" mechanism which enables us to deal with threatening situations. In Helen's case, there was no danger. She was working at her desk is a corporate setting, surrounded by co-workers. Just another day. However, this was to be the beginning of a very difficult but freeing journey of fear, self-imposed imprisonment, and eventual freedom and recovery.

Agoraphobia

Agoraphobia literally means "fear of the market place." In reality, it is a marked fear of becoming incapacitated (fainting, vomiting, losing control of one's emotions, dying) in a public place, or alone, where help may not be available, or where escape is not possible. There is a strong fear of making a fool of one's self during the incapacitation. Common public places which are feared by agoraphobics are crowded places (can't escape), public transportation (can't get off in time), bridges (can't get off quickly), tunnels (stuck), highways (can't get off between exits), elevators (can't get off between floors), churches (crowded), restaurants (eating in public is sometimes difficult due to fear of choking or looking stupid), and high-rise buildings (can't get down quickly). As you can see, all of these places have one thing in common: they are difficult to leave from quickly.

"There were several situations that induced fear in me. The most difficult were sitting in church, standing in line in any store, especially the grocery store, driving on a highway, and being above the first floor of any building. I had a much greater chance of panicking in these places if they were full of people."

She told me of her first panic attack.

"I'm sitting in a crowded church during Mass. I am looking around, seeing all the familiar faces from my hometown, and my parish priest is standing at the pulpit. I sense the enormity of the church in comparison to myself, the 'almightiness' of it all . I feel so small and insignificant. I feel faint, my heart is racing, and I begin to sweat. I need desperately to leave. I know that if I can just get outside, I will be safe and in control of my body. But I feel so trapped. There are people on both sides of me in the pew. In order to get out, I would have to climb over their legs, squeezing my feet in the tiny space between the seat and the kneeler. There is no way I can get out without causing a disturbance. My panic increases and I think for sure that God will take me right there."

"I began to avoid places in which I had actually had a panic attack, such as my work place, church, and driving on the highway, as if the places themselves were dangerous to me. Gradually, however, I began to stay away from more and more situations since I could always find some sort of relationship between the current setting and a place where a panic attack had occurred. I finally reached the point where I feared I would die if I even walked out of my three room apartment to get the mail. My only safe place was home."

Panic attack + Anticipatory Fear + Avoidance of Place = Agoraphobia

Anticipatory fear is a common cause of panic attack. The fear of helplessness or of losing control in a given situation often causes the person to avoid the place of the last panic attack, *as if the place were the culprit.* The avoidance becomes a safety precaution, but creates the new problem of agoraphobia.

When Helen first experienced her panic attack and resulting agoraphobia, she felt frightened and embarrassed. She first consulted medical doctors. She thought it would be more socially acceptable to have a physical problem than a psychological disorder. Each year, thousands of men and women are mistakenly diagnosed, given unnecessary medication, and remain untreated. Tranquilizers only mask the problem. But there is help.

The medical community so far knows that there is an apparent biological component in panic attacks and agoraphobia, as it tends to run in families. There is a high incidence of eating disorders prior to the onset of panic attacks. Studies have shown that there is a higher incidence of traumatic early life events, such as maternal separation, parental divorce, or trauma before the age of four. The average agoraphobic is female, with the problem surfacing by age twenty-six. Certain anti-depressants are quite effective in treatment. But studies have shown that medication and psychotherapy combined are the most effective treatment.

In Helen's case, she chose not to take medication. She feared the side effects, although there are relatively few with today's "serotonin re-uptake inhibitors." The assistance of medication would have made her progress so much easier and quicker, but she feared everything.

At first, our work took place over the telephone. Although we first met in person, it became increasingly difficult for her to get to my office. She was afraid to drive and couldn't arrange for transportation. It soon became apparent that she was completely afraid to leave her house.

Although traditional therapy consists of weekly fifty-minute sessions, I spoke to Helen daily on the telephone, from ten minutes to one hour per day. The consistent contact made it possible for an on-going relationship to develop, one of trust and concern. Sometimes it's necessary to throw away normal methods, choosing instead what feels right for each particular circumstance. Twice a week therapy is better than twice as good, in terms of growth and healing. The continuity is clearer. Daily interaction is boundless in its ability to heal. In five months, Helen went from being home-bound to returning to work full-time.

When working with panic attacks, I use a method called **systematic desensitization**. It exposes the patient to the cause of anxiety in a safe and limited way. For example, she was afraid to sit outside on her porch. On day one, I advised her to open the door and look outside. On the second day, she would open the door and lean outside. On the third day, she would step outside. On the next day, she would linger outside. On the next day, she would sit down outside. On the next day, she would sit down and stay outside for awhile. During all of these attempts, she would practice abdominal breathing **(see Appendix 2)** which mechanically slows down metabolism and induces physical calmness. Obviously, everyone's timing and anxiety is different. On some days, she would be able to do more than others. She would also be able to remain calmer if certain people were with her. We called these people her **safe people**.

I also recommend listening daily to a relaxation tape **(See Appendix 1)**. Systematic desensitization and relaxation techniques greatly relieve *symptoms*, but it is just as important to treat the *cause*.

Fear Index

During a panic attack, I find it helpful for the person to grade the fear on a scale of 1-10, where 1 is calm and 10 is a feeling of imminent death. Aside from giving the person something else to think about, it identifies the severity and duration of the attack. In the beginning, one may experience a 9. One minute later, it may lessen to a 5. Later in treatment, one may only experience 6's. It's helpful to keep a notebook of all attacks, noting the location, time, and circumstances. Progress can be charted with accuracy.

Panic Attack Notebook

Date/Time	Location	Fear Index #	Circumstances

I have noticed in my practice that every agoraphobic or panic attack patient I have worked with has also suffered from repressed anger at the same time. As the anger is expressed and released, the number of attacks lessen until gone.

And so, what Helen and I focused on primarily was her relationship with her husband. They had been married for three years following a two-year courtship in college. Although he loved her very much, he had a very bad temper and was angered rather easily. Helen, on the other hand, was very passive and sweet, completely unable to stand up to his loud outbursts. She reacted by not reacting. She became very quiet and docile. Of course, the anger and hurt that she felt had to go somewhere. She repressed it, suppressed it, and told herself that she was OK, until it came out in the form of panic attacks.

Your body never lies.

In Helen's case, her body is what got her to my office. Her marriage was in trouble, she had been depressed and angry for years, but always told herself that she was just fine. How often do we say that?

"I'm fine...I'll be OK...As soon as this is over, I'll be able to take some time off for myself...I don't have time for me now..."

We lie.

Everyday sometimes. We tell ourselves we're OK. But your body never lies. It is simply not sophisticated enough to know about denial of the truth. If you're doing too much, it will make you tired. If you're stressing yourself, neglecting yourself, or simply not taking care of yourself, it will make you sick.

Your body is brilliant. It will make you sick until you stop to give yourself the time and attention and care you need to heal yourself.

Symptoms of Anxiety & Stress

* Headaches
* Stomach ailments
* Muscle aches
* Irritable bowel syndrome (colitis)
* Insomnia
* Panic attacks
* TMJ pain (temporal mandibular joint)
* Chronic Illness
* Frequent Accidents
* Difficulty Concentrating
* Difficulty Focusing
* Irregular Menstrual Cycles
* Forgetfulness

And so, Helen's body gave her panic attacks when she was holding onto anger. She had repressed her true self for too long. As she learned to release her anger in an appropriate and assertive way, in a **Quietly Powerful** way, her need for panic attacks ended. And her panic attacks ceased.

Anger turned inward is depression.

Helen's Father's Programs:

"Do what you're told."
"Take abuse."
"You don't deserve to be treated with respect. "
"You deserve to be yelled at."
"Alcoholic drinking is normal."

Helen's Mother's Programs:

"Be quiet and obey your father."
"You are not important enough for me to protect you from your father's anger."
"My marriage to your father is more important to me than you are."

Helen had been mildly anorexic as a teenager. Often, an eating disorder is a physical manifestation of feelings of utter helplessness. The anorexic feels no control over her own life. She is never allowed to make her own decisions, and it feels that what she wants just doesn't matter. And so, the anorexic will deny herself food. At least she can control her weight. It's as if she is saying, *"I don't need."* And the bulimic who binges and purges after deprivation is saying, *"I don't need. Yes I do. No I don't."*

When Helen was a little girl, her father was very controlling and judgmental. Although he had been dead for several years, Helen carried his opinions and criticalness inside of her. A concrete example of this was when she spoke of her anxiety and guilt over serving only wine at her wedding reception. It caused her much pain every time she thought about it. She said she was embarrassed at the very idea that her husband limited the bar. I asked her what her father would have thought about the wine-only reception, if he had lived to attend her wedding. She physically cringed when I posed the question to her.

"My father's favorite drink was scotch on the rocks. Can you imagine if he couldn't have had his scotch at my wedding? When I was little, he used to make me be the bartender for him and his drunk buddies. I hated it. I felt so embarrassed and I hated how his friends treated me. It would have been if one day I had said to him, 'No, you can't have scotch. But here's a glass of chardonnay.' He would have killed me."

Once Helen was able to make this connection, her guilt about the wine-only reception completely disappeared.

When the feeling doesn't appear to make sense, and when the emotion is too intense for the situation, it simply means that we need to go back to the Scene of the Crime to find the real cause.

In the course of therapy, Helen read several books on anger and assertiveness and learned how to express her feelings and needs in a Quietly Powerful way (see *The "Quietly Powerful" Exercise*, Chapter 2). This was difficult for her because she feared the loss of her husband's love, but she took the risk. He was surprised at her quietly powerful response to his anger. He had been used to her quiet acceptance of his outbursts. He felt threatened by her lack of fear of his temper, since he had used it to control her in the past. And since he didn't alter his behavior, their marriage did not ultimately weather Helen's growth and change. Helen decided it was more important for her emotional and physical health to rid herself of an abusive relationship in order to be free.

Helen deleted her old painful Programs and rewrote her own:

Helen's New Self Programs:

"I am entitled to express myself."
"My feelings and needs are important."
"I deserve to be heard."
"I am free to be myself."
"I am lovable."
"I make choices for myself with freedom."
"I am lovable and a good person."
"I trust in my own ability to make wise decisions."

Today, Helen is happily remarried and the mother of two children. She wants me to tell you that she is giving them beautiful loving Programs, like she wishes she had received.

I can't remember where I first heard this, but I have always loved the following concept: *"Everyone is born with a worry space. Some people have big worry spaces. Others have small worry spaces. The rule is: The Worry Space Must Be Full At All Times."* So, if you have a big worry space, but only small problems, you must blow up these problems until they become big problems so your worry space will be full. But if you are lucky enough to have been born with just a small worry space, then small problems don't need to get blown up out of proportion, because the worry space is filled so easily. The trick is to try to make your worry space as small as possible. Everyone is predisposed to a certain amount of worry. But you don't have to be at the mercy of the size of your worry space.

How To Stop The Worry Habit

1. **Ask yourself, "What's the worst thing that can happen?" Is that really so bad?**

2. **Notice that most of what you worry about never actually happens.**

3. **Set aside a certain time of day for worrying. Fifteen minutes is often enough time to think about your worries and fears. Try to think of nothing else. If you find you have a worry during the day, set it aside until it is your "worry time."**

4. **Make a list of everything you are worried about. Note which ones are productive (things you can control), and which ones are non-productive (things you cannot control).**

5. **Use "thought stopping." Say outloud, "NO!" whenever you catch yourself worrying. Break the worry habit.**

6. **Replace worry with faith and trust.**

The Mindbody

There are times in our lives when nothing can calm the anxious mind or saddened heart. It is then that I prescribe Meditation, Hydrotherapy, Aromatherapy, Visualization, Audio therapy, and Nutritional therapy. Sounds very complicated. Translated, it consists of taking a warm scented bath in a candlelit room with beautiful music and a glass of wine or sparkling water. All of the senses are soothed. And when we soothe our bodies, our minds naturally follow. Old folk medicine works.

We are made up of **mind, body**, and **spirit**.

The Mind is the thinking self.

The Body is the physical self.

The Spirit is the intuitive inner sense of self.

We feed our Mind with facts from school, television, the Internet, newspapers, and magazines, trying our best to keep up with the events of the world.

We exercise and diet our Body in an endless attempt to control it, to keep it fit and healthy. We go to the gym, jog, cross-train. We eat non-fat low-cholesterol low-calorie food, all so that we can make our bodies conform to the accepted ideal of beauty.

We expand our Spirit in our religious pursuits, community work, and interpersonal relationships so we'll be more loving human beings.

But we are cheating ourselves out of one of the most enjoyable aspects of being human: our Sensuality. We have been so focused on the development and perfection of our mind-body-spirit in the last century that *we have forgotten to enjoy ourselves.*

We have forgotten our sensuality.

Webster's Dictionary defines sensuality as "capacity for feeling, the state or quality of being sensual; fondness for or indulgence in sensual pleasures."

The five senses of sight, touch, taste, smell, and hearing (and the sixth sense of intuition) are given to us to perceive the world around us. In our race to be perfect, we have forgotten to smell the roses. We allow ourselves to live under stressful conditions and accept it as normal. It doesn't have to be that way. We work to be able to live. Do you live to work?

Nutrition-Exercise-Rest

I cannot say enough about the importance of taking care of your body, especially when under stress. Because of the Mindbody Connection, we need to devote our time and energy into the maintenance of good health and appearance. We have seen how the body can manifest physical symptoms of hidden emotional distress. It works both ways. We can experience emotional symptoms of anxiety and depression if we ignore our physical health.

Our bodies are like machines that need to be maintained with the best of ingredients, much like a finely-tuned car. You wouldn't put low-grade gasoline into a Mercedes. It's the same with a human body. We need a balance of nutrients to feel at our best. Eat well. And of course, optimum weight ensures better health, not to mention happiness when looking into a mirror.

Your heart and soul live inside of your body.

Sometimes the best way to alleviate the physical symptoms is with physical methods. Breathwork is often an effective way of slowing down the body's fight or flight mechanisms. **(See Appendix 3)**. Aerobic exercise, stretching, yoga, and walking are all good forms of exercise which can alleviate symptoms of depression and anxiety. I often prescribe exercise at least three times a week for people experiencing emotional upset of any kind. Try it. It is remarkably effective.

Rest, relaxation, and sleep are necessary for mental health. When we ignore this, we are setting ourselves up for cloudy thinking, lack of concentration, and poor problem-solving skills. You need to be rested to think and feel at your best. Rest. I recommend Relaxation and Self-Hypnosis Tapes for a variety of physical and emotional symptoms of distress **(See Appendix 1)**.

Peter's Story

Tall, dark, handsome, and completely miserable. Peter was twenty-one years old and allergic to food. He had severe reactions to many common foods, such as beans, peas, wheat, and nuts. He had to be especially vigilant in restaurants, because many dishes used small amounts of these foods as filler. Every meal was a potential threat that could instantly cause a violent asthma attack, sometimes resulting in hospitalization.

Peter had his first asthma attack at the age of five. Difficulty breathing, wheezing, closing of the throat, chest pain, rash, and vomiting. Asthma is a chronic lung condition characterized by periodic breathing problems, brought on by allergies, stress, exercise, or weather. The asthma attack can last for a few hours to a few days. In Peter's case, it was an allergic reaction to food.

Peter was tired of being tied to his inhaler, and wanted to be free to eat everything. He somehow believed his condition was psychosomatic, and came to me for advice. We went to the **Scene of the Crime**.

"I was raised in England by wonderful parents who owned a small grocery store in the village. They worked a lot, so I was cared for in the day by aunts until I went to school. When I was five years old, I had a nanny who I liked very much. She would let us play in the kitchen while she baked cookies. There would be about six children there everyday, and we all had fun. But one day, I didn't want to eat my vegetables. The nanny became very angry and instructed her big strong husband to hold me down while she forced me to eat. I felt like I would suffocate. The nanny's husband held my nose closed, while she put food in my mouth. This happened on several occasions, causing me great fear and panic. And then one day, when I was five years old, I had an asthma attack. It scared everybody. And the forced feedings never happened again."

Peter's body had developed a way to avoid the forced feedings. Asthma even mimicked the feelings of suffocation. But now, it was his own body that was doing this to him. It solved the initial problem, but turned into a problem of its own. And seventeen years later, there is no nanny, and certainly no one would attempt to force feed him. Yet Peter's body still carried the defense of asthma.

He had a very severe case. He would develop symptoms if he ate, smelled, *or even saw the beans, peas, or nuts.* He lived in constant fear that these particular foods would enter his sight or land on his plate in a restaurant. He needed to be constantly cautious, and this was exhausting.

Nanny's Programs:

"You have no control over your body."
"You have no say over what happens to your body."
"What you want or don't want doesn't matter."
"You are powerless."
"You are at the mercy of other people."

I decided to use hypnosis to uncover his unconscious beliefs about these foods. I use a lot of hypnotherapy in my work. I see how it speeds up the recovery process by going straight to the inner core beliefs.

Hypnosis

Hypnosis is an altered state of consciousness, an artificially induced state of relaxation which allows for heightened suggestibility. If you've ever arrived home but couldn't remember how you got there, you've been in an altered state, also called trance. Your unconscious self reacted to outer stimuli such as stop lights and other cars, while your conscious self was thinking about something else. During hypnosis, your brain waves are slowed, which allows for an alteration in how you perceive and process information from the environment.

Suggestibility

When we are very young, our minds accept all information as true. We don't have screens to differentiate between truth and non-truth. That's why Parental Programs are so powerful. They are accepted as truth, and remain in our unconscious belief system forever. *Unless they are made conscious.* Freud said the purpose of analysis is to make the unconscious conscious. Hypnosis can help. If we can go into the unconscious mind and find the core beliefs, we can also alter them, delete them, and suggest new beliefs better suited for freedom and happiness.

I explained hypnosis to Peter, and he was eager and willing to do whatever it took to be free from his allergies. I gave him my relaxation tape **"Breathe...As if your life depended on it" (see Appendix 1)** to use for one week prior to our session. I have found that trance is easier to induce in people who have practiced with self-hypnosis and relaxation.

After Peter was in trance, I gently regressed him to the age of five. I made sure that he was *watching* himself at the age of five, making it safe for him to re-experience the events without having to physically re-experience the pain. He merely witnessed the scenes from the safety of being an adult watching himself as a child. I guided him to remember the kitchen, the sounds of the other children, the smell of the food, and the clothing he wore. He visualized the kitchen in detail, and saw his nanny serving the food onto the plates. I then asked him to witness his nanny get mad at him for not wanting to eat his vegetables. A tear rolled down his cheek as he remembered. And then he saw his nanny's husband restrain him as she forced the food into his mouth. He stayed with this memory for awhile, and then I gave him a new suggestion. I told him to see him tell his nanny that he didn't want to eat his vegetables. But this time, she smiled at him with love and said,

"That's OK. You can eat whatever you want. You decide. I want you to have whatever you need to be healthy. You can say yes, or you can say no. You decide." Another tear ran down his cheek. And then I had him see his nanny's husband smiling at him as he offered him all kinds of food. Peter said "yes" to some, and "no" to others. He saw himself with the power to say "yes" or "no." And when the hypnosis was over, Peter left feeling strangely confident and didn't know why. Later that week, he ate a tiny piece of wheat bread, something he could normally not eat. And nothing happened! He experimented with other foods and found the same results.

We had a few more hypnotherapy sessions to reinforce the new Programs given by his nanny in the regression state. Peter noticed that the new freedom translated to other areas of his life. He felt entitled to make choices about restaurants and movies, something he always let others decide. He also found himself fearless on a Ferris wheel, something he'd been too afraid to try in the past. He felt mildly exhilarated with this newly found freedom to eat whatever he wanted. He learned he had the power to decide. He still carries his inhaler, but feels soon he will be able to throw away this old security blanket. He no longer needs the asthma to protect him. He knows the war is over.

Peter's New Self Programs:

"I can make my own decisions."
"I can say 'yes' or 'no.'"
"I have the right to make choices for myself."
"What I want matters."

Mary's Story

When Mary walked into my office, she was ninety-five pounds and thought she was fat. She was twenty-five pounds underweight. Mary was anorexic and bulimic. But she didn't come to see me for therapy for an eating disorder. She was there to resolve a problem with her boyfriend.

Mary was raised in a rigid and controlling family who told her what to do, how to do it, what to say, how to dress, and who her friends should be. They came "from the old country" and didn't want her to make the same mistakes they did. When Mary turned thirteen, she wanted to choose her own clothes and friends, but this was seen as rebellion and not allowed. So Mary unconsciously took control of the only aspect of her life that she could. Her body. Her distorted body image caused her to think she was fat. The bonier she became, the better she thought she looked. Whenever her parents urged her to eat, it only made her more determined to lose even more weight.

Mary's Parental Programs:

"You are imperfect."
"You need us to function."
"You are not capable of making any decisions."
"Good girls obey their parents."
"You cannot trust your own judgment."

Medical Assistance

I always like to have the advice and cooperation of the family physician in problems which are medically related. We can monitor body weight and hospitalize if necessary. Mary and I made a contract that she would maintain her weight of ninety-five pounds with the promise that she would gain weight over the next few months as our work together progressed. If any weight was lost, she would be hospitalized.

Symptoms of Anorexia Nervosa

* **Less than 85% normal body weight**
* **Fear of gaining weight and of being fat**
* **Distorted body image**
* **Loss of menstrual cycles (3 months)**
* **Misuse of laxatives, enemas, diuretics**
* **Excessive exercise**
* **Fasting**

Symptoms of Bulimia Nervosa

* **Binge eating**
* **Feeling a lack of control over eating**
* **Self-induced vomiting**
* **Sense of self based on weight and shape**
* **Distorted body image**
* **Misuse of laxatives, enemas, diuretics**
* **Excessive exercise**
* **Fasting**

Whenever I work with an eating disorder patient, it is important for me to deal with the underlying feelings of helplessness, powerlessness, and hopelessness. Mary had become dis-empowered by her well-meaning, over-protective parents. They loved her very much, and only wanted the best for her, but they were robbing her of her growth. Mary needed to **separate and individuate** from them.

At twenty-nine, she reminded me in many ways of a nineteen year old who needed to go through the normal adolescent stage of learning who she was in order to become her true self. We go from children who need our parents to teach and guide us, to teenagers who move from dependency to independence. Mary never got that far.

In our work together, she learned she had been making lots of decisions on her own without realizing it. She had worked as a computer analyst for years, and had received praise from her supervisors. She had had a relationship with her boyfriend for two years, although she kept this a secret from her parents. And she had decided to enter into therapy on her own too.

Guilt & Shame

Her biggest problem was guilt and shame. She believed if she went against her parent's wishes, she would be "a bad girl". She felt dishonest, ashamed, unable to function on her own, and disloyal. For example, Mary would rather feel guilt and shame rather than face the fact that her parents had maybe been too overbearing with her. She still needed to idealize them. It was necessary for Mary to find her own inner power and sense of self.

The "Guilt" Exercise

*Purpose: * To remove a useless, draining emotion*

I feel guilty when...

I resent the fact that...

I want it to be OK for me to ...

It's OK for me to...

Complete the sentences for a situation that makes you feel guilty. By writing this exercise, you may achieve a better sense of your true feelings, which may not include guilt at all. You may uncover hidden anger and resentment, or fear and anxiety. It's best to know what your real emotions are.

Mary's Guilt Exercise:

I feel guilty when I think about moving out on my own, and making my own decisions. I feel that I would hurt my parents terribly.

I resent the fact that I'm twenty-nine years old and still living at home.
I resent the fact that my parents treat me like a nine year old and tell me what to do.

I want it to be OK for me to move out on my own and have a normal grown-up relationship with my parents. I want them to respect me and love me for who I am.

It's OK for me to move out and make my own decisions. My parents may be hurt and angry at first, but hopefully they will realize that it's for my own good. I need to do what is right and healthy for me.

Shame is a belief in one's own guilt.

Guilt is a belief in one's flawed self. Guilt leads to self-blame, and shame is beneath self-blame. The answer to this unhappy cycle is to examine the validity of the guilt. Misplaced guilt is often unexpressed anger. One way to separate guilt from anger is with *The Guilt Exercise*.

As our work continued, Mary became more empowered. She made lots of self-discoveries and learned to trust in herself. As she became more able to make decisions, her eating disorder was no longer necessary. Her body grew in direct relation to the sense of control she felt in her life.

Food and Shopping

I have noticed that an eating disorder is often accompanied by a tendency to shop excessively. Over-eating or buying to excess can have the same underlying cause; to fill the emptiness inside with "stuff" from the outside. Food, clothes, cars. I had an obese patient who told me that a new sweater made him happy for two hours, a new a new car for two weeks, and a new house for two months. He knew it was time-limited, and sensed he longed for something more than an outside "fix." Once there is a connection made, we can learn to look elsewhere for answers. Remember, the solution to the vase with the hole in the bottom is to fix the hole, not to add more water.

So Mary learned that she didn't need food to fill the empty space she felt inside. And she didn't need to deprive herself to make herself perfect. She looked within and wrote new Self Programs and learned to live by them. She filled herself with herself. She got an apartment with a girlfriend and broke up with her controlling boyfriend. She maintains a normal, healthy body weight. She and her parents are working on their relationship, which could take some time.

Mary's New Programs:

"I manage my own life. "
"I control my destiny."
"I am capable."
"I am able to make good decisions."
"I am lovable."
"My opinion and what I want matters very much."
"I deserve..."

Your Turn

Look into yourself now, and learn what your body is telling you. ***Questionnaire 5: Are You Healthy?*** will help you to identify any health issues that may be psychologically related or caused by emotional distress. ***The "Write & Draw Like A Child" Exercise*** will help you to find hidden ideas and beliefs known to only your unconscious self. And Homework *4: Meditation* will give you a lifetime tool for relaxation and peace.

Questionnaire 4

Are You Healthy?

1. What were some of the health issues that you had as a child? Did you have frequent colds, sore throats, ear infections, or allergies?

_____

_____

_____

_____

2. How do these same health issues occur in your adult years?

_____

_____

_____

_____

3. Can you see a relationship between health issues and your emotional state?

_____

_____

_____

4. How much time do you spend on your health? Diet, exercise, vitamins?

_____

_____

_____

_____

5. In what part of your body do you physically experience anxiety? Depression? Disappointment?

_____

_____

_____

_____

6. Where do you hold your tension? Shoulders? Neck? Stomach?

_____

_____

_____

7. Does anyone in your family suffer from Clinical Depression? Anxiety? Mental illness of any kind?

_____

_____

_____

_____

8. Is there a history of alcoholism or drug addiction in your family?

_____

_____

_____

_____

9. Describe your own use of alcohol and drugs, past and present.

_____

_____

_____

_____

10. Do you ever eat when you're not hungry, just to soothe yourself?

_____

_____

_____

_____

11. Do you sleep well? Do you ever awaken very early in the morning, unable to fall back to sleep until six or seven a.m.?

_____

_____

_____

_____

12. Do you find yourself using alcohol or drugs to soothe yourself?

_____

_____

_____

13. What could you do right now to improve your overall health?

_____

_____

_____

_____

_____

_____

_____

_____

_____

_____

_____

The "Write & Draw Like A Child" Exercise

Purpose: * To uncover unconscious fears, beliefs, and ideas

Take a large piece of paper and fold it in half, width-wise, separating the left and the right side of the page. If you are right-handed, write a question with your right hand on the right side of the paper. Ask for insight into yourself or a problem that has been bothering you. If you are left-handed, write with your left hand on the left side of the paper. Now, answer the question on the other side of the paper with your other hand, your non-dominant hand. It may feel awkward and difficult, like when you were a child first learning how to print. But you will be amazed at what you write.

We have insight, unconscious wisdom, and knowledge that can be accessed with this method of writing. This method allows access to the other side of the brain. Use it whenever you need more than conscious knowledge.

Whenever you feel blocked or unable to make a decision, you may also draw a picture of the problem. Draw like a child with crayons and pencils. Sometimes we have no words for feelings or situations, but we can visualize the concept. Look at your drawing, and sometimes it will illuminate your solution.

Homework 4

Meditation & Prayer

Take time every day to stop everything. Meditate for 20 minutes every morning, and pray for 20 minutes every evening. Praying is asking for what you want. Meditation is listening for the response. It will change your life. If you haven't been trained in a meditation technique, such as Transcendental Meditation, I offer a method in **Appendix 2** which is based on the focusing on your breath.

Insights

_____

_____

_____

_____

_____

_____

_____

_____

_____

_____

_____

_____

_____

"The meeting of two personalities is like the contact of two chemical substances: if there is any reaction, both are transformed."

C.G. Jung, from "Modern Man in Search of a Soul" 1933

Chapter Five

Compatible Couples

I see a lot of couples in my practice, and I marvel at how their deepest core issues play so perfectly with each other. We seem to choose someone who will touch our most painful places. I saw a sign once that said, "Opposites attract, then opposites attack." What initially attracts us to our mate is exactly what drives us crazy after a little time has passed. After romance has turned to realism, eyes are opened and the truth can be seen. The "gregarious out-going man" is later described as loud and intrusive. The "responsible, organized woman" is later viewed as rigid and unbending. How sad. The truth is, we choose each other because of the lessons we are able to teach and receive. We are all teachers and students of each other, especially in a romantic relationship. It is the place of greatest learning and joy, or the greatest misery and suffering.

It is our goal to find our differences, see the extremes, and find the inner balance. We need to strive for the middle common ground, the place of moderation and simplicity. For example, if the wife is neat and fastidious, and the husband is messy and sloppy, they are put into each other's lives, not to drive each other crazy, but to learn how to be more like the other. She needs to learn how to be less perfectionistic, and he needs to learn how to be more organized and focused. They need to meet in the middle. Balance.

Look at your own relationships and see what bothers you. *Instead of trying to change people to be more like you, your truth lies in learning how can you can be more like them.* If two people do this together in a relationship, it gets rid of blame. It creates growth, understanding, and harmony.

I believe we are unconsciously attracted to someone who possesses characteristics we need to develop in ourselves.

The Four Seasons Rule

I believe it is important to know who your partner is before making a commitment. It sounds obvious, doesn't it. If you had to choose only one platonic friend for the rest of your life, you would make sure this person had all of the traits of a good friend. You would take your time to make this decision. If you had to choose a business partner for life, you would make sure this person had all of the qualifications needed to meet the needs of the company. But somehow, when it comes to choosing a mate, we sometimes don't take the time to see who the person really is. It's so much more fun to be swept away with the romance, wine, and song. Remember the old proverb, "Marry in haste, repent in leisure."

New love emerges in the Springtime. Love intensifies during hot Summer days. In the Autumn, we begin to fall away from idealism, and the Winter darkness can be difficult to weather. In four seasons, we experience all aspects of a relationship.

I strongly recommend **The Four Seasons Rule**. Know someone for at least four seasons before you make a commitment of forever. Anyone can be nice for a few months. When you spend a year with someone, you see how they react to all kinds of situations. You see their true nature in good times and in bad. It's especially good to know the bad. The whole key to a good relationship is knowing how to resolve conflict. There will always be disagreement and discord, to some extent, because two people are individuals with unique personalities. If you can resolve problems with respect, honesty, and simplicity, your relationship will last.

The quality of the relationship is determined by the ingredients of the people involved.

An extraordinary meal is created by an experienced chef who uses the finest ingredients. No matter how skilled the cook, if the ingredients are not fresh and ripe, the meal will be mediocre at best. It's the same in relationships. Both people have to bring quality and integrity to each other for success.

Communication Styles

Much has been written in the past decade on the differences between men and women. We are definitely different. What matters most is the ability to accept these differences for the sake of understanding. When I hear women wishing their husbands would listen better, be more nurturing, and talk more about their feelings, I tell them they are describing a woman. Men and women need to be more accepting of the differences, because there lies the attraction.

Linda's Story

Linda reminded me of Lucy Ricardo. She had Clairol-red hair and a look of mischief in her eyes. She'd been married for twenty-three years to an evil version of Ricky. She described him as being verbally abusive and physically threatening.

"He was controlling, demeaning, sarcastic, and very derogatory. He beat me two or three times a year, just enough to keep me in line, but not often enough for me to leave. But there was always the threat of another beating. That was just as scary for me. And then he'd be charming and sweet. He never beat the children. But I hated when they saw him hitting me. That wasn't right."

She withstood this abuse until she learned he was seeing another woman. Even then, she tried to reconcile with him, unsuccessfully.

"I was so torn between my love for him and my hate for his abuse. It seems hard to believe that even today, I think of him and feel an ache for him. Why would I want to be with a man who calls me stupid and says I'm not a good wife? He ignored me when I needed him. I feel like I raised the kids alone. I was so good to him. I took care of him. I loved him. At first, he loved me too. I think it was after we had the kids when he stopped paying attention to me. I kept trying to make him love me, to talk to me, to treat me right. All I got was black eyes. I had lots of great sunglasses. My friends never knew the physical part because I was too embarrassed. I think I was also protecting him. I wanted them to like him. I loved him too much. If only I could have been stronger, I would have left sooner. But by the time I was finally able to leave him, my self-esteem was zero. Another woman. I just couldn't stand it anymore. I hated him."

Linda was suffering from clinical depression when I met her. She hadn't slept in weeks, couldn't concentrate, and felt an overwhelming sadness.

Hate is the dark side of love.

It is amazing how quickly emotions change from love to hate. It's nature's defense against pain. It's a protection from feeling overwhelmed with grief. But eventually, the pain has to be faced.

Symptoms of Depression

* Feelings of sadness, tearfulness
* Diminished pleasure or interest in normal activities (anhedonia)
* Decrease or increase in appetite, weight loss or gain
* Insomnia or hypersomnia
* Restlessness, or slower movements
* Fatigue, loss of energy
* Feelings of worthlessness, hopelessness, guilt
* Difficulty in concentration, decision-making, thinking
* Inability to focus
* Thoughts of death or suicide

Anti-Depressant Medication

When we're depressed about a stressful event or situation for an extended period of time, our bodies are physically exhausted and can become unable to maintain an adequate amount of serotonin or dopamine in the brain. This neurotransmitter controls mood, and when depleted, can result in an emotional and physical depression. It's a downward spiral. What starts out as a depression over a life circumstance can evolve into a physical condition. Emotional depression can create a physical depression, which calls for a physical solution. That's why anti-depressants like Prozac work so well. It simply supplies the serotonin that the body is too weak to make for itself. And when the person feels stronger and recovered, the anti-depressant is no longer needed. Sometimes people are born with a chemical imbalance, a shortage of serotonin. Anti-depressants can then be used for basic maintenance (Remember Daniel's Story, Chapter 2). I don't often recommend medication. However, in the case of an extended clinical depression, I find it to be a valuable tool to help the person regain strength and the ability to think clearly.

A homeopathic alternative to anti-depressants is Hypericum perforatum, also known as St.John'sWort. In the best-selling book "Hypericum and Depression" written by my friend Dr. Harold Bloomfield, studies on Hypericum have found it to be as beneficial in the alleviation of depression as allopathic anti-depressants. Everyone's chemistry is different; medical advise should be sought to help you decide what is best for you.

Combatible Couple

Linda had several of the above symptoms for the past eight months since her divorce was final. I referred her to a psychiatrist for a medical evaluation. She was placed on Zoloft, one of the newer SSRI anti-depressants.

In some ways, Linda would acknowledge the abuse was wrong, but in other ways she felt she deserved it. She was quick to defend "Ricky" and liked to tell me stories about how good he was with the kids. She never defined his treatment of her as abusive behavior until she saw a similar situation on "Oprah."

"There was a woman describing her marriage on national TV, and it sounded like mine. Except she kept calling it abusive. And everyone agreed! I was shocked! It had never occurred to me that I was being abused. It felt so normal to me, I guess because I was raised that way."

Why would an intelligent, rational, attractive woman allow herself to be placed in this situation of daily abuse? Linda was taught that she was not worthy of love and respect. She can remember being beaten by her father in the presence of her mother, for no reason except that he was in a bad mood.

"My mother would say, 'Please stop, you don't have to hit her.' Mostly, I remember thinking how feeble her attempts sounded to me, even as a child. She was too afraid of losing him, I guess. So she sacrificed me. I didn't matter."

Here, at the **Scene of the Crime**, Linda learned that she deserved to be beaten, that she wasn't worthy of love and care and protection.

Linda's Father's Programs:

"You are unlovable."
"You are bad."
"You deserve to be abused."
"It's OK for me to use you to vent my hostilities."

Linda's Mother's Programs:

"Take the abuse. You deserve it."
"You are not worthy of my protection."
"You are bad."

And so she believes it. Her relationship with her ex-husband resulted in abuse, confirming in Linda's mind that her parents were indeed right. She didn't see her role in choosing this type of man who would abuse her. **A self-fulfilling prophesy.**
Linda had the following dream:

"I'm trying to grow my hair because I think I will be prettier and everyone will like me better. Every time it gets to a certain length, I look in the mirror and it's back to being short. Once, I had no hair at all. I kept trying to protect my hair, to let it grow, and nothing I did worked.""

Linda's dream clearly expresses her profound sadness and frustration about trying to win the love of her father and later her husband by making herself "better." In her dream, she is trying to be as pretty as she can be, but can't succeed. Something always gets in the way. She feels **not-good-enough.** Notice she was trying to be prettier to gain approval and love.
Linda's therapy consisted of returning to the **Scene of the Crime** to learn how she lost her self-esteem. She saw her Parental Programs: *"You are unlovable and deserve abuse. Take the abuse."* She was then able to review her dysfunctional relationships with abusive men and saw how she had obeyed her Programs through the years of her marriage. Later, she was able to write new Self Programs to regain her self-love and feelings of worthiness. And she walked away from abuse.

"I am lovable and deserve to be treated with respect and love."
"I surround myself with loving and giving people."

This is not a speedy process. Recovery from trauma and abuse takes time and healing. But it doesn't have to take years. Making connections between childhood and the present makes sense out of life, and frees one to make better decisions. When we understand the drama that repeats, we are free to stop the madness.
Finding the **Scene of the Crime** is imperative if we are to have self-understanding. The coping techniques we learned as a child made sense at that time and most likely worked. But not anymore.

The behaviors that worked in childhood to protect us are often the very behaviors that cause difficulty in our lives today.

For example, a neglected child that becomes a caretaker for her younger brother because of the absence of a responsible parent learns an appropriate life-saving coping mechanism. However, if she continues to sacrifice her own needs, neglecting herself out of habit, this same behavior is now hurtful to her.

Cycle of Violence

The following description of abuse and violence has been adapted from the Domestic Abuse Intervention Project in Diluth, Minnesota (tel 218.722.4134).

A man can exert Power and Control over a woman by using:

Threatening Behavior:
Physically threatening to hurt her or loved ones
Threatening to leave her
Threatening to commit suicide

Intimidation:
Making her scared by actions, gestures, looks
Making her scared by destroying property, displaying weapons

Emotional Abuse:

Demeaning her

Lowering her self-esteem

Name-calling

Calling her crazy

Mind games

Inflicting guilt and pity

Isolation:

Keeping her away from her friends and family

Keeping her at home

Controlling what she reads, how she spends her time

Minimizing, Denying, and Blaming:

Denying the extent of the abuse

Blaming her for his behavior

Macho Behavior

Treating her like a maid

Acting like the "master" or "king"

Making all the decisions because "he's the man"

Financial Abuse

Controlling all the money

Keeping her dependent on him for money

Preventing her from earning her own money

Keeping her unaware of the family financial situation

A Healthy Relationship Is Based On Equality:

Communication

Safe, non-threatening conversations and arguments

Woman expresses herself with comfort

Respect

Non-judgmental listening and talking

Understanding and support

Valuing her opinions and ideas

Trust

Supporting her goals

Wanting her to have her own friends, activities, beliefs

Honesty

He accepts responsibility for his behavior

He communicates with honesty and integrity

Home Responsibility

Fair distribution of work in the home

Financial Responsibility

Both partners make money decisions together, both benefit

Dick And Jane's Story

Jane is a twenty-eight year old adult child of alcoholic parents. "A really good girl." A good student, a good employee, a good patient; always on time, agreeable, easy-going, and eager to please. These are often characteristics of an adult who tried to stay out of the way in a chaotic childhood situation. *"Don't call attention to yourself. Blend. Stay out of the way. Be perfect so you won't be punished."*

She initially came to therapy to ease out of a hurtful relationship with a man who gave her little time or attention. She had wanted to get married and have a child, but her boyfriend always put her off, postponed decisions about their future, and kept her hanging on.

"I saw him sporadically for three years. I would rearrange my schedule at the last minute to make myself available to him. He was always too busy to take time for me. I always felt unimportant. I would give him an ultimatum and he would throw me a scrap, some sign of love or attention. But

finally, I couldn't do it anymore. After I realized that it was going nowhere, I ended it. It was better to be alone than alone in a relationship."

Jane grew up in a home of chaos and drinking. She learned that if she didn't take care of herself, no one would. She became completely independent and self-sufficient by the age of eleven. She was given Parental Programs that would lead her to future relationships of neglect.

Jane's Parental Programs:

"You're on your own."
"Take care of yourself."
"You are not worthy of our time or attention."
"We're too busy for you."
"It's your responsibility to take care of us when we're drunk."
"Everything is your job."

And so she was attracted to this man who gave her little attention and made her feel unimportant. She had learned well how to take care of herself last and others first. She catered to his every need, hoping to win his time and attention. Their time together consisted of her listening to him, about his work, his problems, his ideas. In other words, she had put herself last in her relationship, always attending to his needs at the expense of her own. Classic co-dependent behavior, to use an over-used phrase.

My friend Teresa humorously calls co-dependent people "Tontos". We all remember the Lone Ranger. He received all the glory and the fame. But he had a faithful sidekick named Tonto. We don't really know too much about Tonto, except he was always there to help save The Lone Ranger when he got into trouble. We seemed to understand intuitively that the Lone Ranger needed him. But Tonto thought his role was to be the silent helper in the background. He never spoke up as an individual, and didn't receive credit for being a hero, either. Jane was Tonto.

Enter The Lone Ranger.

Dick is a forty year old recovering alcoholic who is the president of a large corporation. He came to therapy two years ago in the beginning of his sobriety to learn how to effectively deal with anxiety and a dysfunctional marriage. He had lived in a ten year marriage of convenience while he was drinking. His insecure wife never bothered him or demanded anything from him. Their intimate relationship had ceased to exist after the first four years, and both were hanging on for security.

With his recovery from alcohol, the dynamic of alcoholic/co-dependent was gone, and their marriage resulted in divorce.

He was a very high-functioning alcoholic, even at the worst point in his drinking life. No one ever would have suspected, as he limited his drinking to Friday through Sunday mornings. But when a DUI was made public, he finally felt the motivation to quit. His embarrassment and humiliation served him well. He attended AA meetings regularly, worked his Program daily, and made great progress in his recovery.

When Dick and Jane met, they had both deleted their Negative Parental Programs. He was in recovery from alcoholism, and she was in recovery from co-dependency. Perfect timing.

Jane and Dick are a perfect example of two people who had extracted themselves from dysfunctional roles in past relationships, and appeared to be ready to choose more appropriate partners. Unfortunately, as their relationship progressed, each fell into their past known behaviors. The first few months were quite romantic and whirlwind. They moved in together very quickly and married one year later. (They obviously didn't follow the Four Seasons Rule.) During their courtship, Dick was dealing with his divorce, a stressful situation at work, a DUI, a new relationship with Jane, and a move to a new house. He had a hard time dealing with all of the changes, but didn't want to slow down the pace. Jane was very supportive during this time, but sensed his anxiety. Her urge to jump in and rescue him was almost overwhelming their marriage. With all of this stress in their lives, both reverted into past, comfortable roles. Dick withdrew, not being able to express anger or disagreement in a constructive manner. His withdrawal spurred Jane to pursue him, to over-function, and she felt neglected. A familiar feeling.

Both Dick and Jane expressed dissatisfaction in the area of communication. Jane easily talks about her feelings, while Dick is often unaware of his feelings and finds it impossible to express them to Jane during times of conflict. Dick explains:

"Sometimes, I have a vague feeling of anxiety or anger, but I can't seem to connect it to an event or reason. I just know that I feel bad. But in my family, when I was little, we weren't allowed to be angry. My parents could be angry and yell, but we weren't supposed to feel bad. I guess I sort of forgot to know when I'm angry. And even if I'm able to understand the reason I'm upset, I don't want to tell Jane because I don't want to hurt her feelings. I'm also afraid of sounding stupid. I'm just not good at this. I guess my Program of "Don't feel anything bad" doesn't work too good in a relationship. The problem is, I do feel bad. I just don't know why or what to do about it."

Dick learned as a child to repress his natural and healthy desire to express anger or discomfort. This is a very common complaint.

"I wasn't allowed to get mad. You just don't do that in my family. I was taught by the nuns that anger is a sin. Anger is unbecoming. No one likes you if you're mad all the time. So I just keep it to myself. Of course, I feel like I'm going to explode. Sometimes I do. I yell and scream and I scare myself."

Dick's Programs:

"Don't get angry. Anger is a sin."
"Pretend all is well."
"Ignore your feelings."
"Drink if you feel bad. It takes away the pain."
"You don't have to take care of yourself. Someone else will take care of you."

And so Dick learned a valuable coping technique. He disowned his anger. He even became unaware of it after awhile. And by not expressing his anger as a child, he stayed quiet and docile on the outside. This kept peace in the family. He wasn't yelled at as much because he played the role of the "good little boy." *The very thing we do as a child to save ourselves is the very thing that hurts us as an adult.* Dick's inability to express anger or talk about negative feelings created a major problem in his marriage to Jane.

Jane learned to be the placater in the family. When her parents would drink, she would take care of them. When they withdrew from her, she would try to do even more for them to get their attention.

"What really bothers me is that Dick shuts down when something is bothering him, and there isn't anything I can do to get him out of it. I never know if he's mad at me, or work, or what. I hate it. Sometimes it goes on for days. He doesn't talk to me, or he'll snap at me. I don't know what to do to make it better. He's slipping away from me."

Prognosis for this relationship doesn't look good. Dick has relapsed recently and is blaming Jane for his feelings of anger and depression. He doesn't appear to be willing to look at his "escape" behaviors - shutting down, withdrawal, and drinking. He stopped going to AA meetings and therapy. Jane is taking the caretaking role. She explains away his relapse, not completely understanding the significance. She seems to be tiring of this familiar role, but feels paralyzed. Neither wants to look at their own issues at this time. Both are making their Programs true, again. He is feeling ashamed because of his hostility towards her, and she is feeling abused and abandoned by his alcoholic behavior. What started as a loving relationship gradually turned into repetition of the past for both. A tragic relapse into old Negative Programs.

Your Turn

Questionnaire 6: Are You Ready To Learn? will help you to look at your own relationship with new eyes. Step outside of yourself and see the couple you have created. If you're not in a relationship now, look at your past. When you do ***The "Jack & Jill" Exercise***, be honest. You may be surprised at what you learn. And ***Homework 5: Find A Mentor*** will greatly speed your process of growth and change.

Questionnaire 5

Are You Ready To Learn?

1. How would you describe your relationships?

_____

_____

_____

_____

2. Does your mate remind you of anyone in your family?

_____

_____

_____

_____

3. How does your mate make you feel about yourself?

_____

_____

_____

4. How did your parents make you feel about yourself when you were little?

_____

_____

_____

_____

5. Are these feelings similar? In what way?

_____

_____

_____

_____

6. What role do you take in your relationship?

_____

_____

_____

_____

_____

7. What role did you take in your family as a child?

_____

_____

_____

_____

8. Are these roles similar? In what way?

_____

_____

_____

_____

9. Describe the perfect parental marriage.

_____

_____

_____

_____

_____

10. Describe your perfect marriage.

_____

_____

_____

_____

11. Describe your parent's marriage.

_____

_____

_____

_____

12. Describe your marriage/relationship/past relationships.

_____

_____

_____

_____

13. Are you repeating your family's relationship styles in your own relationships?

_____

_____

_____

_____

14. What can you do to change your Relationship Program?

_____

_____

_____

_____

_____

_____

_____

_____

The "Jack & Jill" Exercise

Purpose: * To understand the male and female parts of ourselves

There are certain traits in our society that are seen as masculine and feminine. Masculinity is often paired with aggression, decisiveness, logic, rationality, and control. Femininity is often described as soft, gentle, romantic, sensitive, and nurturing. Every man has a feminine aspect in his personality. C.G. Jung called this the *anima*. Every woman has a masculine aspect in her personality. Jung called this the *animus*.

I believe we need to connect to these parts of ourselves in order to better understand our male-female relationships. There are really four of us in every couple: the male self, the feminine-male self, the female self, and the masculine-female self.

Let's call the feminine-male self **Jill.**
Let's call the masculine-female self **Jack.**

Let's look at an example. Sue and Leonard are having an argument. She doesn't understand why he doesn't make more money, and keeps asking him why he doesn't get the promotion. Leonard yells back that the company is having hard times and tells Sue to get off his back. But, if we look inside Leonard and Sue, we find **Jack and Jill**. Sue's **Jack** is aggressively fighting for what she thinks Kenny deserves; that is, more money and more respect from a better job title. Leonard's **Jill** is feeling inadequate and embarrassed because his wife sounds like she's belittling his present income and profession. Both are misunderstood. If Sue and Leonard are able to identify the **Jill and Jack** in each other, this knowledge would lead them away from argument and take them instead towards support, understanding, and compassion. Sue would be able to support Leonard's job frustrations, and Leonard might be encouraged by Sue's belief in him to go after more.

Find Your Jack and Jill

Look inside and identify your other self. You may be aware of this already, but often, the other-gender self is disowned. By disowned, I mean not valued or not liked. Girls have been warned to not act like boys, and boys are teased if seen at all girlish. Both genders have positive and negative aspects. It is in identifying and owning all parts of ourselves where we will find our wholeness and our richness.

Next, look at your mate's other-gender self. Find the characteristics that may be hidden. Discuss this theory with each other. In knowing the **Jack and Jill** within, understanding each other should come easier. Support each other in your other genders, and during times of disagreement, try to speak from your **Jack and Jill**.

Bring all of you to each other.

Homework 5

Find A Mentor

I want you to find a mentor to guide you towards success and happiness. A mentor is someone who is usually older, wiser, and more experienced, who can help you along the way to your goals. If your goal is personal growth, find a spiritual teacher. If you want a better marriage, consult someone whose marriage you admire. If you want to be more financially successful, seek out an entrepreneur. In other words, you don't have to reinvent the wheel. Find a mentor who has "been there" and "done that." Your mentor could come in the form of a self-help book or biography. Let yourself receive guidance from someone who is where you want to be, who has achieved what you want to have.

Insights

_____

_____

_____

_____

_____

_____

_____

_____

_____

_____

_____

_____

_____

"There is always one moment in childhood when the door opens and lets the future in."

Graham Greene, from "The Power and the Glory" 1940

Chapter Six

A Complete Internal Work-Up

The following stories illustrate how looking into our childhoods can illuminate why we do the things we do. We make the same mistakes again and again. We go down the same bumpy road and expect to end up somewhere new. Instead of looking outside for the answer, we now can look inside our Programs.

Karen's Story

"I was sexually abused by my uncle when I was six to eleven years old. I don't remember all the details, but I think intercourse started when I was about eight. The only reason it stopped was because I got my period."

This is how Karen started our first session. She was bursting to tell someone what she had never told before. She didn't cry. She hadn't been able to have feelings about her memories. She just "knew" she was bad and disgusting and dirty.

Karen's Programs:

"You are a sexual object."
"Your worth comes totally from your sexuality."
"No one takes care of you or protects you."

Karen was a dancer at a strip club and a high-priced prostitute. Had she had a different childhood, her beauty would be seen in a feature film co-starring Mel Gibson, not in pornographic movies. A high percentage of prostitutes and strippers have been sexually abused as children. One call-girl told me that she had *never* met a "girl in the business" who hadn't been sexually abused. They were taught that this is where their value lies. Without their sexuality, they feel worthless. And *because* of their sexuality, they feel worthless.

I noticed that Karen always dressed very provocatively. Her neckline was low and her skirts were high. Make-up was heavy. Tattoos and rings were present but not visible when dressed. She took time to sexualize her appearance, even if she were only coming to see me.

"I feel like my only redeeming quality is my sexuality. I know I'm sexy, and I'm good at what I do. I just feel so demeaned when I do it. I want to stop, but I make thousands of dollars every week. I have no other skills, and I couldn't live on minimum wage. Who would hire me anyway."

Karen's boyfriend added to her low self-esteem. He met her at a strip club and reminded her that he dated her in spite of that. Already, he treated her as inferior. She accepted this because she believed it too.

In our work together, I first had to help her see her true self, apart from her sexuality. As an experiment, I asked her to dress in a conservative, non-sexual way for one week. When she did this, she at first felt invisible and worthless. Then she started to notice that people were still nice to her, and in fact, women were nicer to her than ever before. (Surprise.) She started to find an identity apart from her sexuality.

She also never made the connection before between her work and her sexual abuse. Of course she would choose a profession that focused on her sexuality. It's the only arena where she felt competent, useful, worthy, and successful.

When we talked about her sexual abuse, she was finally able to find the feelings of guilt, shame, fear, and pleasure that she had as a child. She especially felt guilty about the pleasure. It's common to feel special, loved, and aroused during molestation. When she learned her responses were normal, she was relieved. I asked her to write a letter to her uncle, who had since passed away.

The letter gave her a feeling of power as she expressed her anger and pain. When she read it to me, she cried tears of power, release, and freedom.

We processed her feelings and memories for months, until her pain turned to compassion and understanding for herself.

Karen's New Self Programs:

"I am worthy."
"I am more than a sexual being."
"I am a whole person."
"I deserve to live a normal life."
"I deserve a loving relationship and respectable work."

Joy's Story

Joy is the kind of mother who makes other women feel inadequate. Besides being beautiful and in shape, she bakes cookies and homemade bread before working an eight hour day. Her five children are honor roll students, and Joy is active in the PTA. How does she do it? She takes no time for herself. At forty-two, she had never stopped to live her own life. She was a wife, a mother, a daughter, and a friend, but she wasn't ever just "Joy."

Daughter of an alcoholic and gambler father, oldest child of three, she learned at an early age that she would have to take care of herself and her younger brothers. Her mother was often drunk when she came home from school, and would yell at her for no apparent reason. Her father was mostly absent, either at work or at the track, gambling what little money there was. Often, there was no food. Her parents were a product of the Depression. They taught her scarcity and fear. They were advocates of "Spare the rod, spoil the child." It's what they were taught, and they were passing it down.

"There was craziness in my house, all the time. My father was drunk a lot, and I was my own parent from the time I was six. I learned that if I were very quiet and passive, my life would be easier because I would become 'invisible' and wouldn't be noticed. If you're 'not there', you can't get into trouble. I was smart. I was the 'good little girl' so I wouldn't get yelled at or beaten. It's amazing how easy it became to be whoever they wanted me to be. Also, I knew I had to take care

of my brothers. If I didn't, no one else would. They were my responsibility. I somehow always knew that. And so I went without."

Co-Dependency and Stress

This childhood programmed a woman to be extremely responsible, reliable, and independent. And mistrustful. However, she is also very co-dependent in her dealings with everyone. "Co-dependency" is an over-used word that simply means putting others' needs ahead of one's own, at too great a cost to the giver. A co-dependent person is so busy buying shoes for her family that she doesn't even know she's barefoot.

Joy originally came to therapy because she felt her depression was interfering with her ability to be a good wife and mother. Notice that her depression was not her primary motivation. That was second nature for her. I remember our first session vividly.

"My life is out of control. I'm so unhappy and I don't know why. I have a wonderful husband, great kids, a perfect life. And I feel like running away. What's wrong with me? Why am I so depressed?"

In the first few sessions, it quickly became apparent that she was clearly focused on everyone else's life and needs, with little awareness of her own.

"And who takes care of you?" I asked one day. She looked shocked, as if that question had never entered her mind. She burst into tears and replied, *"No one, not ever."*

Through our work, she came to understand that her over-giving behavior was a natural method for her to deal with the world since that's what she was "taught" as a child. Her co-dependency led her to put her family's needs ahead of her own, taking care of their lives and leaving her own to chance. She had no real understanding of her own needs and feelings, nor did she feel she had a right to even have them. Remember, she was also an "adult child of an alcoholic". She didn't know what "normal" was. She was so accustomed to feeling stressed, it was her "normal" state. She had many symptoms of anxiety (see Chapter 7). The first step was for her to recognize her stress level, and to learn what caused it. I asked her to keep a **Stress Journal**. In using this tool for one week, she was able to identify the people and situations that increased her stress level.

Stress Journal

Day	Time	Situation	Feeling

Knowledge of the problem offers the solution.

One of the first goals in our work together was to define her needs and her self-identity. This was not easy for her. She felt selfish at the very idea of taking the time to focus on herself. In fact, she felt guilty for allowing herself to continue in therapy.

In order to make sense of the present, it was necessary to look at her self-esteem issues by connecting them to her Scene of the Crime.

History

Remember the **Scene of the Crime,** the times we are "taught" in childhood that we are unworthy of attention, love, affection, and general care. If the parent is alcoholic and unable to care properly for a little girl, she doesn't have the intellectual or emotional capability to say, *"I am worthy of love and care and I am not getting it because my parent has the disease of alcoholism."* Instead, she blames herself for being unworthy of that care because of the need to idealize the parent. If a little boy is being mistreated or abused by a rageful parent, he doesn't think, *"My father is abusive and I do not deserve this."* He instead feels, *"If I were lovable and good, these bad things would not be happening to me. I must deserve this."* If a dysfunctional parent verbally abuses a child by name-calling or derogatory remarks, the child believes the statements to be true without question, and later has difficulty seeing himself through realistic eyes.

If someone tells you everyday that you have purple hair, eventually you will look into the mirror and see purple highlights.

Starting Over

I believe it is the aim of the therapist to "re-parent" the patient with love and respect, empathy, and understanding. The role of the therapist is to teach the patient to look into herself with unbiased eyes, not through the eyes of the dysfunctional parent. Often there is an unwillingness to do this, an unconscious need of the patient to protect the integrity of the parent. We are left with a dilemma: *"If I am really lovable and good and deserving, then my parents were wrong and incapable of giving me what I needed,"* versus *"My parents were right and I am unlovable and bad and undeserving."* I believe that re-parenting and acceptance by the therapist is necessary for growth and freedom to occur. In the case of Joy, after going back to the Scene of the Crime, she saw that that's where she learned to de-value herself. She was able to connect this to her over-doing behavior of the present, and was able to redefine her own needs, her relationships, and her self-esteem.

Joy is learning to value her self, honoring her own individuality and needs. While she still has the responsibilities of being a wife and mother, she is also learning to focus on herself and to care for herself at the same time. She *is no longer last in her own life.* She has realized that she has neglected herself for too long, and that it's her job to take care of herself in the same giving, loving, special way that she offers to others. And her hardest lesson of all is to ask others for help. She continually works on her sense of deservingness.

"I now host a weekly women's group in my home. Expressing myself with other women with similar lives helps me to feel empowered. I no longer feel alone, and I value their friendship. I have also learned that my husband is not a mind-reader. It is my responsibility to tell him my feelings and needs. He isn't able to love me in a way that feels completely comfortable for me, but at least we're on the right track. To tell you the truth, he isn't used to me expressing a need of my own. I have to teach him that I'm here too."

It is by achieving a love for herself that she will be free to live her life with balance and happiness.

Joy's New Self Programs:

"I am here and I matter."
" I am important."
" I am special. I am lovable.""
"I have needs and desires and wants that matter."

Ben's Story

Ben was a forty year old gay computer programmer with extensive experience and talent as an actor and singer. At the time of our first session, he was working in a corporation instead of a theatre because he wouldn't allow himself to pursue a career in entertainment. That was not his **Vocational Program**, as you will see.

Although he felt no conflict about his homosexuality, but was unable to tell his parents, even though he thought they suspected. Ben thought that his lifestyle was beyond their realm of acceptance or understanding. Fortunately, Ben had been able to accept his sexual identity from the time he reached young adulthood. The earlier the self-acceptance, the easier it is to live as a minority, even with discrimination and negativity.

Ben came to therapy wanting to get unstuck in his career. He felt paralyzed to make the leap from programmer to performer. We discussed his Scene of the Crime and learned his Programs.

Seeing the daunting Programs on paper that have been unconsciously dictating his professional choices gave Ben the clarity he needed to grow and change.

Ben's Father's Programs:

"I think my father really didn't have a strong Program for me because he had no real identification with me as I became an adolescent, then a young adult, and now an adult. My mother always used to tell me that I reminded my father of himself when he was young, in many ways; I looked like him and had many of his qualities. I never asked her about the qualities partly because I never really envied anything about him that I already didn't have. I came to a significant understanding about him at a very young age, fourteen or fifteen, and never really expected more. I know he really loved me, even if he didn't have an emotional way of showing it. That brought me an understanding, coupled with sadness, which allowed me to forgive him and to continue to love him. His Vocational Program and Personal Program for me was to have a career as a corporate executive, with a wife and children. Like Darren on 'Bewitched.' He never gave me the option of not having a traditional family. Mostly, I felt a vagueness from him, and therefore I was left with a vague sense of myself."

Ben's Mother's Programs:

"I see her as a weak, yet wise, somewhat pathetic old woman who is cheating herself of a great potential old age. She started too late in life to respect her body and her spirit, and remained tied to the earth, the day-to-day of life, and got caught in the minutia. I find it hard to identify with her as the young, energetic, Marlboro-smoking woman who dictated major portions of my youth. She really must have been an emotional blanket of insecurities and world fears. I remember one example; checking and re-checking to see if the doors were locked, throughout the day, even though we lived in a suburb that felt like Disneyland. How crazy. I guess I just remember her as more manager than nurturer, although I do remember some lovely, close moments, so I know I was given an idea of what the better things were. In other words, I knew what I was missing when I was missing it.

"My mother's Program for me was that I was going to be a dynamic salesman. She really had big designs for me as a money-making corporate type. She never understood why I wasn't happy in the nine-to-five world and to this day she asks me why I don't get a permanent job in the department I'm currently working in. My response is usually, 'If I were going to be a corporate type, don't you think it would have happened by now? I didn't spend thousands of hours in the theatre to be a schlep in some insurance company.' She doesn't want to hear my choices, my own Programs. She wants her own to be realized. For quite some time, I have known that the reason she wants me to fill her Programs is because she can then not have to worry about me. I'll have money, I'll have security, I'll have her generations' American Dream. It's interesting, almost incredible to have led a life that lies at the end of your street or on the other side of town, without ever wondering what's on the other side of the world. She thrived on safety, on sameness, and her Program is wanting 100% of the same for me."

Ben's difficulty was in giving himself permission to not follow his Parental Programs. It's clear that he was on the edge of obeisance, never fully committing to working the nine-to-five corporate life. But he hadn't been able to commit to the pursuit of an entertainment career either. He had been in over one hundred musical productions in well-respected theatres, and had received countless offers of assistance to further his acting career. It was interesting to watch him straddle the corporate and entertainment Programs. Having never fully committed to either, he had never fully achieved success in either.

It's clear from his story that not everyone complies with their Programs. However, where there is non-compliance, there is usually a sense of holding back, an idea of fear of success, of actually having what one is striving for without really understanding why.

During our work together, as he saw his Programs, he was able to gradually break from the corporate world completely.

"I think divorcing myself from her insecurities and fears is really the key. As I go through life, I really feel her fears eating into me. These are not my fears, but rather the ones I grew up listening to. I really have a great sense of self and life and its gifts. I just need to take the parent off my shoulder. I am so different from these people called my family, but I have always liked the sense of not belonging as much as I've liked the feeling of belonging. I want to be accepted by the world. But I want it to be with my own terms intact, on my ground. None of this total nine-to-five compromise."

Ben's New Self Programs:

"Successful well-known actor-singer-songwriter"

I am certain you know him.

Your Turn

So now, take Questionnaire **6: Look Around** to see yourself as strangers do. The **"Get Amnesia" Exercise**, if done with honesty and detachment, will move you towards believing your new Programs. See yourself as if for the first time. And **Homework 6: Group** will offer an arena for sharing your work with others.

Questionnaire 6

Look Around

1. Describe your physical appearance.

_____

_____

_____

_____

2. Describe your clothing.

_____

_____

_____

_____

3. Describe your home and furnishings.

_____

_____

_____

_____

4. What kind of food is in the refrigerator?

_____

_____

_____

_____

5. Are there plants, animals, children?

_____

_____

_____

_____

6. What kind of music do you own?

_____

_____

_____

_____

7. Are there messages on your telephone answering machine?
   Are there photographs of people, or
   other signs of interaction?

   _____

   _____

   _____

   _____

8. What do you do for work? Do you like it?
   How are you paid, treated?

   _____

   _____

   _____

   _____

   _____

   _____

9. Who are your friends? Several, or few? Close, or acquaintances?
   Similar to you? Equal or needy?
   Do you have mentors?

_____

_____

_____

_____

10. Are you married, single, in a relationship?
    Happy, satisfied, functioning well?

_____

_____

_____

_____

_____

_____

_____

11. How do you spend your time? How much work, how much play?

_____

_____

_____

_____

12. What did you learn about yourself by doing this exercise?

_____

_____

_____

_____

_____

_____

_____

The "Amnesia" Exercise

Purpose: *To see yourself clearly,*
                 as if for the first time.

By now, you should have a pretty good understanding of your own Programs. Hopefully, you have thought about them, written them down, analyzed how you made them true, written new Self Programs, and figured out how you will make them true. But here's a way to speed things up a bit: *Get Amnesia*.

Remember in the film "Spellbound," Gregory Peck has amnesia and is searching for his identity, for his past? Can you imagine what it must feel like not know who you are, where you live, what you do for work, who your family and friends are? It must be terrifying, *but it also must be freeing.*

If there is no memory, there can be no knowledge of Negative Programs.

I know nothing

I often ask my patients to **Get Amnesia.** They are often so entrenched in their past that they can't see their present. Their sense of self is based on their Negative Parental Programs. So one way to get rid of Negative Programs is to forget them. *Forget everything.*

Look in the mirror. What do you see? See yourself as a stranger sees you. Look at your features. Don't just take for granted that you actually know what you look like. What do you like? What don't you like? See your face and your body as if for the first time. What's your best feature? Smile. Relax and look. *Really* look. How do you dress? Do you like your clothes? Do you take care of your appearance?

Now, look around. Where do you live? What are your surroundings like? Look in closets and drawers. Who is this person who lives here? Are you living in a place that's comfortable, neat, disorganized, soothing, modern, messy, clean, noisy, dark, filled with art, plants, children? What kind of environment have you created for yourself?

Where do you work? Are you successful? Are you in a position that feels healthy and productive? Is your job satisfying? Who are your co-workers? What kind of relationships do you have with them? How does your boss see you? Are you doing well? How do people treat you?

And most importantly, who are the people in your life? What are your relationships like? Do you have a few close loving friends, or do you have many light, casual acquaintances? Are you married to someone you love, or are you stuck in a bad relationship? Would you choose these people all over again? Are you surrounded with good, kind, happy, loving, supportive friends and family? Have you let destructive and negative people into your life? How do your friends and family treat you? Are you loved? Are you close to your family? How often do you socialize? What do you do for fun? Do you have fun? Is your life balanced between love and work?

As you assess your life through the eyes of someone with amnesia, you will become aware of your self in a new way, with a new perspective. By getting amnesia, you are allowing yourself to see the life you have chosen for yourself. You will see yourself without the negativity that so often surrounds you if you are still entrenched in your Negative Programs.

Lisa's Story

Lisa is a thirty-seven year
old ghostwriter of best-selling biographies. With red hair and porcelain white skin, her appearance is striking. Her parents owned a florist shop, which meant long hours and hard work. When she was a baby, her parents placed her in a flower box in their shop as they worked, and she was often told she looked like a delicate little flower. Lisa remembers feeling invisible, blending in with the arrangements, waiting for her parents to take her home.

Lisa's Parental Programs:

"Blend."
"Be invisible."
"Wait."

How She Made Them True:

Professional ghostwriter
Relationship with married man.

Ghosts Are Invisible

It's strange but understandable that Lisa grew up to ghostwrite books for other authors, never receiving credit for her own work. Invisible. And her ten year relationship with a married man completes the rest of the Program: *look pretty, and wait.*

Lisa wrote out her Programs and was fascinated with how the whole process worked. She quickly had a major breakthrough, and became quite depressed when looking back on how easily she had blended and remained invisible. When you're busy blending and being invisible, you don't know who you are. So Lisa did **The Get Amnesia Exercise**, and told me she was surprised at what she learned. When she looked in the mirror, she saw a red-haired petite, slender, pretty woman, the same good-looking woman who appeared in photographs around her apartment. The clothes in the closet reflected a sense of style that would be worn by a fashionable yet conservative businesswoman. Photographs on the wall showed she had an abundance of friends; she seemed to always be the center of attention. Her place was tastefully decorated with a warm lived-in look. The CDs showed a mix of classical music and modern jazz, while the books included topics of history, romance, and cooking. She told me, in amazement, *"I guess someone smart and pretty lives here, someone popular. Is that me?"*

Having stepped away from her everyday ideas of who she was, she was able to take a good look at herself. She was *surprised* to learn that she was pretty. She was *surprised* to learn that she had great writing ability. She was *surprised* to learn that she was surrounded by lots of wonderful people who loved her. **The "Get Amnesia" Exercise** was an important ingredient that enabled her to see herself. As I write this, she is looking into the idea of writing her own book under her own name. And needless to say, she is a little tired of waiting for the married man, a little tired of living a cliché. No longer willing to blend or to be invisible, Lisa has begun her journey to find her true self.

Homework 6

Group

"Once a week, we come together to share ideas and feelings. We whine, cajole, support, cry, and laugh with each other."

People in group share their feelings, but sometimes they're only sharing what they think is socially acceptable. Sometimes they use a "bad" word or talk about their desire for an affair, but mostly they *pretend* to be free to say who they really are. If they *really* said what they felt and presented who they are, they would be relieved and scared to death at the same time. Relieved because they would be the same, and scared because they wouldn't trust they were all the same. And by the same, I don't mean the same personality. I mean their sameness would be their humanity, their uncertainty, their vulnerability. We sometimes have a wonderful capacity to trust, to share, to communicate. But sometimes we say:

"No, I need to keep this to myself. She is thinner-smarter-happier-in a better relationship than me so I can't be my true self with her."

We can take our Parental Programs and place them before each other and give them up. Or we can choose to make them true and hide behind them. Love or fear. Decide.

Form a group. Neighbors. Friends. Acquaintances you wish were friends. Complete strangers from an ad in the newspaper. Weekly, monthly. Meet in a home. Have tea and cookies, or pizza and beer. Be together. Practice being who you truly are. Let this be the stage where you audition. The group can be formed around similar issues and backgrounds: a Parental Program group, women's group, survivors of incest, assertiveness training, stress-management, relationships group, parenting group, weight control group, a 12-Step Program. Or it can be a random collection of people with nothing in common except a desire for growth and change.

Learn each other's lives. Be each other's therapists. Go to the Scene of the Crime. Find your Parental Programs. Write them on paper. Help each other write New Self Programs. Help each other choose freedom.

Insights

_____

_____

_____

_____

_____

_____

_____

_____

_____

_____

_____

_____

_____

_____

"There is a place in you where there is perfect peace. There is a place in you where nothing is impossible. There is a place in you where the strength of God abides."

A Course in Miracles 1975

Chapter 7

Re-Program Your Relationships

At the **Scene of the Crime**, we are given **Parental Programs** that dictate our relationship choices.

"You will have abusive relationships because you are unlovable."
"You will have loving relationships because you are lovable."
"You will have no relationships because you do not deserve to be with anyone."

There are countless Programs, limitless results.

If a woman was raised by an alcoholic parent, she will most likely have relationships with alcoholic men. One might expect her to avoid the alcoholic because of the emotional pain she endured as a child. However, it's exactly the opposite. **We are drawn to what feels "normal" and "comfortable."** This is not to say that this woman *likes* abusive alcoholic behavior; she is merely *used to it*. She has a history with the scenarios, the chaos, the crazy behavior. It is known to her. A woman who has no experience with alcoholism in her life would not be able to relate to alcoholic behavior and would be less likely to tolerate it. A woman who was yelled at by an angry mother would find herself in relationships with angry men. It would feel comfortable, in a familiar way. A woman raised by an emotionally distant father would be attracted to a workaholic. She would feel right at home with her feelings of neglect. It doesn't matter if the new relationship doesn't exactly replicate the childhood facts. What is repeated is the *feelings* of abuse, neglect, unworthiness...

We call this **repetition compulsion.**

We are unconsciously compelled to repeat the negative situations and feelings of childhood.

This is why we often find ourselves in the same scenarios over and over again, just with different people. It's been said that "insanity is repeating the same behavior and expecting different results." It's time to become sane by identifying the underlying disruptive Negative Programs.

Cynthia's Story

The first time I met Cynthia, I was impressed by her professional attitude, air of confidence, and stylish designer clothes. At forty-four, she looked and acted like a career woman with everything going for her. But she surprised me when she took a deep breath and said, *"I have no life. Everyday, I go to work, do my job, come home, put on my bathrobe, sit on the couch, and watch TV."*

Cynthia was addicted to marijuana.

She didn't tell me at first. She was too ashamed. She made me guess, and when I did during our first session, she was shocked. But what else but addiction would explain her self-inflicted isolation and loneliness?

She was a child of the 60's, when everyone got high and it was cool. Except when everyone else stopped and "got a life," Cynthia kept on going. She moved to California in search of sun, drugs, peace, and love. She found it all, and the drugs became the focus of her life. But her friends left and she hid her drugs because it was no longer "politically correct", and that left her at home alone on the couch with a TV and a joint.

"By day, I am responsible, controlled, capable, and good at my job. No one would guess. And at night, I am nowhere."

She was terrified the first day she came into my office. She had tried to quit drugs on her own, countless times. She'd be strong in the morning, but by the afternoon, getting high was all she could think about. She had heard that marijuana was not addictive. She knew it was. She wanted to stop, but she didn't know how.

Normally, I don't work with anyone who is still using drugs. It doesn't make sense to work with someone who is deadening pain with a drug. I tell them to come back when they're clean and sober. But I intuitively knew that it would be ludicrous in this case. Cynthia was in my office for help, and she needed reassurance and hope before she would be able to give up *her* version of reassurance and hope. I agreed to see her unconditionally. High or straight. I only asked that when she saw me, she would be straight.

I decided my focus would be her self-identity, apart from marijuana. I knew that if our success in therapy focused on her abstinence, it would not occur. Cynthia needed to feel acceptance and love from the outside before she could give herself acceptance and love on the inside. We looked at her **Scene of the Crime**.

Cynthia's father was her love, her idol, her everything. She was "Daddy's little girl" until he abandoned her when he was hospitalized due to a sudden onset of depression and erratic behavior. During his mental illness, he spoke only to her. Doctors would reach him by speaking to him through her. And later, when he recovered enough to divorce and remarry, he disowned her, not wanting to be reminded of his painful past.

Cynthia's mother at this time became a very successful business woman in order to provide for her. But Cynthia didn't care about the financial assets. She only wanted the attention her mother was too busy to give. And so she felt abandoned by both parents.

Cynthia's Parental Programs:

"You are on your own."
"We will not shield you from pain. Deal with it."
"Be hard. You can take it. You don't need anyone."
"We need you to take care of yourself, and sometimes us."
"It might look crazy at home, but we are a fine upstanding family."
"Don't tell anyone about our lives."
"Deaden your pain with drugs and alcohol, like we do."

Cynthia didn't want to be on her own. She didn't want to feel different or isolated or abandoned or hard. So she found a method of deadening the pain. Escape with drugs. When she joined in the druggie group at school, she found immediate acceptance. She felt she belonged for the first time in her life. And it was wonderful not to feel bad anymore. Drugs worked.

Cynthia had a biological predisposition to drug addiction. Her father had been chemically, emotionally imbalanced and her mother had used pain killers to excess on several occasions. Her paternal grandfather was an alcoholic. The biological component coupled with the emotional pain yielded a predictable result: Addiction.

There is a genetic, biological, chemical predisposition for alcoholism and drug addiction if there is a history of alcohol/drug abuse in the family.

When Cynthia returned to the Scene of the Crime, it was very difficult for her to admit her pain existed. She'd been in denial for so long that she had a need to keep the family fairy tale intact. It was important that I let her work at her own pace, not mine. I sat with her, week after week, listening to her fond memories of childhood. And when she was ready, she began to talk of her disappointments, hurts, dissolutionments, and her idealized-abandoning father. When she was ready, discoveries were made. Painful, and freeing.

Recovery

When we met, Cynthia was using marijuana, alcohol, and valium. Her "drug of choice," her favorite drug, was marijuana. She often wondered how she would live without its anesthetizing effects. She used it to soothe herself, to block the emotions of sadness and anxiety.

Symptoms of Anxiety

* Heart palpitations
* Rapid heart beat
* Dry throat and mouth
* Tightness in the chest
    or stomach
* Increased perspiration
* Tensing of muscles
* Gritting/clenching of teeth
* Shortness of breath
* Inability to concentrate, focus
* Urge to run away, escape,
    or hide
* Urge to lash out
* Tired, exhausted,
    lack of energy

* Trembling
* Nervous tics
* Stuttering, speech difficulty
* Frequent urination
* Insomnia/excessive
    need for sleep
* Headaches
* Change in weight/appetite
* Accidents
* Decrease in productivity
* Confusion
* Increased drug/alcohol use
* Increase in illnesses
* Feeling spacey, dizzy, weak

All emotional growth and maturity ends when drug/alcohol abuse begins.

Cynthia had no coping tools for dealing with bad feelings. While other teenagers experienced problems and difficult situations and learned how to cope by developing problem-solving skills, Cynthia deadened herself with drugs.

Emotional growth ends when addiction begins. A person who started abusing drugs or alcohol at the age of fifteen may be forty-two years old biologically, but only fifteen years old emotionally. However, growth and maturity begins again with abstinence. One can age pretty quickly to catch up to adult status with the help of a good AA Program, therapy, or spiritual guide.

Alcoholics Anonymous

After much coaxing, Cynthia finally agreed to go to **Alcoholics Anonymous**. She never considered herself to be an alcoholic, although she'd drink a lot of vodka when she couldn't risk the detection of pot, like on an airplane. She also didn't want to go to AA because she never felt comfortable in crowds. She feared she wouldn't belong. I told her there's no such thing as a purist anymore, and most people are addicted to drugs *and* alcohol. After all, alcohol is just a liquid drug. And everyone who walks into an AA meeting for the first time feels the same; *different.*

One night after work, she finally got up the courage to go a meeting with a friend in recovery. She immediately felt welcome. *She was the same as everyone in the room.* She knew she belonged. And yes, she did become free of all drugs, three years ago. Luckily, she had a "high bottom." She didn't need to lose everything before she quit. Her loneliness and isolation were enough to bring her to therapy and to AA.

I had told her in the beginning of our work together that I saw her as a future leader in AA. I was able to see her as she truly is, without fear. I saw her as an inspiration to others. And that's who she is today. Many meetings and 12 Steps later.

When the pain of using is greater than not using, recovery will begin.

We are both grateful that she chose life instead of fear. Alcoholics Anonymous is a life-saving group that teaches how to live in the real world of pain, joy, success, and failure. As Bill Russell once said, "I prefer to experience life as it presents itself."

The 12 Steps of Alcoholics Anonymous

Step 1
"We admitted we were powerless over alcohol -
that our lives had become unmanageable."

Step 2
"Came to believe that a Power greater than ourselves could restore us to sanity."

Step 3
"Made a decision to turn our will and our lives over to the care
of God as we understood Him."

Step 4
"Made a searching and fearless moral inventory of ourselves."

Step 5
"Admitted to God, to ourselves, and to another human being the exact nature of
our wrongs."

Step 6
"Were entirely ready to have God remove all these defects of character."

Step 7
"Humbly asked Him to remove our shortcomings."

Step 8
"Made a list of all persons we had harmed, and became willing
to make amends to them all."

Step 9
"Made direct amends to such people wherever possible,
except when to do so would injure them or others."

Step 10
"Continue to take personal inventory and when we were wrong
promptly admitted it."

Step 11
"Sought through prayer and meditation to improve our conscious contact with
God as we understood Him, praying only for knowledge of His will for us
and the power to carry that out."

Step 12
"Having had a spiritual awakening as the result of these steps, we tried to carry
this message to alcoholics, and to practice these principles in all our affairs."

Cynthia is now living with a man she met in the Program six months ago. Together they are working on their issues of intimacy and authenticity. And when she is ready, she'll decide if he is the right person for her greatest growth and happiness.

In our male-female relationships, we are at our most dysfunctional and vulnerable. This is the stage where our Parental Programs are played out. This is the place of fastest and deepest growth, and therefore, the most painful. We often choose someone who allows us to re-experience the pain and disappointment we felt as a child; repetition compulsion. But when we get free from our Parental Programs, we can choose to experience the love and kindness we have longed for by picking someone who can share our lives and love in true intimacy.

Cynthia's New Self Programs:

"I am lovable."
"I am open and soft. "
"I need other people in my life."
"It is safe to need."

And she aspires to live it every day.

The Serenity Prayer

God grant me the serenity to accept the things I cannot change, the courage to change the things I can, and the wisdom to know the difference.

Your Turn

Questionnaire 7: Are You An "I" Or A "We"? will help you see if you can hold onto your identity in an intimate relationship. *The "Pie" Exercise* offers perspective on the time in your life. *The "Letter" Exercise* may be used to free up old resentments and hurts. And *Homework 7: New Developments* urges you to grow just a little bit more.

Questionnaire 7

Are You an "I" or a "We"?

1. Are you more aware of your own needs, or your mate's needs?

_____

_____

_____

_____

_____

_____

2. Are you happier when you're with your mate than any other time?

_____

_____

_____

_____

_____

3. How much time do you spend with your mate?

_____

_____

_____

_____

4. Do both of you have outside interests and friends of your own?

_____

_____

_____

_____

5. How much recreational time do you spend together?

_____

_____

_____

_____

_____

6. Would you rather be with your mate than with anyone else? Do you cancel plans with others if you unexpectedly can be with your mate?

_____

_____

_____

_____

7. Do you define yourself in terms of other people? Wife, mother, boyfriend?

_____

_____

_____

_____

8. Is your work meaningful to you? Does it bring you a sense of self, apart from your relationship?

_____

_____

_____

_____

9. Do you go on separate vacations? Do you often not see each other for days at a time?

_____

_____

_____

_____

10. Do you feel like you could go on if something happened to your mate or to the relationship?

_____

_____

_____

_____

11. Is your relationship the most important part of your life? Does your mate have similar priorities?

_____

_____

_____

_____

12. Are you able to argue and hold your own opinion if you believe you are right? Do you often submissively agree just to end a conflict?

_____

_____

_____

_____

13. Do you feel equal in the relationship?

_____

_____

_____

_____

14. Do you find yourself saying, *"We think...."* more than *"I think...."* ?

_____

_____

_____

_____

_____

15. In your life, have you mostly been in a relationship, or on your own?

_____

_____

_____

_____

16. Are you able to entertain yourself and enjoy your own company when you are alone?

_____

_____

_____

_____

17. Do you love your mate freely, or does a part of you believe you need your relationship to function?

_____

_____

_____

_____

18. If something happened to end this relationship, would you want another mate in the future?

_____

_____

_____

_____

19. Do you feel more valuable when you are in a relationship? Do you feel more vulnerable or unstable when you are single?

_____

_____

_____

_____

20. Do you have a strong sense of self when you are with your mate?

_____

_____

_____

_____

The "Pie" Exercise

Purpose: * To learn if your interests agree with your time

Remember when your third-grade teacher had you draw a pie with slices for play time, school, TV time, and family time? You had to fill in the areas of your life, according to how you spent your time. I want you to do that now.

Draw one big circle, and fill in the spaces with how you spend your day. This is called your *Time Pie*. For example, if half your time is spent at the office, that would fill half your pie.

Work, spouse/significant other, children, parents, friends, commute to work time, alone time, hobby, sports, TV. These are some examples of how you may spend your time.

Now, I want you to draw a pie that shows your interests, where your heart is. This is your *True Self Pie*. If your family is the most important part of your life, make it a big piece of your pie. If work is meaningless and unenjoyable, make it a tiny slice. Or vice versa.

Now, look at your two pies. Do they match? Are they even close? Ideally, we are spending our time doing the things that are the most important to us. So, for example, if family is important, but work fills most of your *Time Pie*, you're in trouble. The happiest people are spending their time doing the things they love to do. Use this tool to re-prioritize your life. Make changes where possible. Make a plan to harmonize your life.

The "Letter" Exercise

Purpose: **** To express negative feelings
in a productive, safe way.***

As adults, we can look back on our childhoods and see the Scene of the Crime, the point in time when our Negative Programs were installed. We try to understand that our parents were doing the best they could at the time. But sometimes, our feelings of anger and sadness are overwhelming. We want to express these feelings, but we don't know how.

Shakespeare's Lady MacBeth said, *"Give sorrow words; the grief that does not speak whispers the o'er-fraught heart and bids it break."* Alcoholics Anonymous assures us that saying something out loud takes its power away. Often we feel better just having "gotten something off our chest," regardless of the response. *The expression itself is healing.*

We need to find a simple way to talk about our past hurts and disappointments, *with the person who did the hurting and disappointing.* Sometimes this isn't possible, as when the person is deceased. Sometimes it's not advisable, as when the person is unable to understand. And sometimes, it's simply not in our best interest, as when there would be negative consequences.

And so I suggest a letter. Letter writing can be a cathartic and liberating experience. It can be written, re-written, edited, filed away, thrown away, burned, mailed, or hand-delivered. Whether you choose to have the person read it or not is entirely your decision. Let your actions be motivated by a desire to heal, however, not to injure.

Letters are a slower and calmer method of confrontation than speaking in person. Writing allows you time to gather your thoughts, to feel the anger or sadness in privacy. The completion of the letter is sometimes enough to exorcise the negative emotions you may have carried for years. But sometimes, you may choose to mail it. You may want the person to know on a deeper level what your feelings are. You may want reconciliation, resolution, or understanding, as in Annie's case.

Annie's Story

Annie is a thirty-four year old mother of two boys, ages two and four. She came to therapy at the request of her husband of five years, venting a great deal of anger and frustration.

"I'm trying to be a good wife and mother, but I'm losing my temper every other minute and I feel like I could explode. My husband says I'm a different person now, and the tension between us is growing. Ever since we had kids, I've become more and more stressed, more and more unhappy. I adore my children, and my relationship with Ted is usually great. But lately, I can't explain why I'm so angry all the time."

It's not unusual for a woman's childhood issues to surface after the birth of her own children. It's only natural that she would remember what it was like for herself as a child, to notice the similarities and differences in the care she *received* compared to the care she *gives* as a mother. And in Annie's case, the differences were enormous. Annie was an only child. She describes her mother as "efficient."

"She always made sure I had good clothes to wear and food to eat. All of my physical needs were met. But there was no physical affection in my family. Not even between my parents. My father was at work a lot. He was nice, but I didn't really have much contact with him. He was rather passive, come to think of it. He let my mother decide everything. He never disciplined me. And then they got divorced when I was six."

Annie was sexually abused by her paternal grandfather at the age of seven. It happened on three different occasions. Finally, Annie told her mother. Nothing happened. Annie's mother chose to ignore the situation, thinking it would go away.

Annie's Programs:

"You are not special. "
"You are not safe. "
"I will not take care of you."
"You are unworthy of our protection.
"Your anger and pain is not important."

The Letter

In the course of treatment, Annie wrote the following letter to her mother:

"This isn't to hurt you, but to help us both. It's time we cleared the air and really understood each other. I know you don't understand the anger and rage inside me, but I think I finally do. It started way back in my childhood and the situation with Grampa. It was such a terrible and invasive thing he did and I can remember you telling me, 'It's not that bad!' It was that bad! If someone did that to one of my sons, I would kill them! I don't care who it was, I would protect my child at any cost! I felt completely unprotected by you. For years I thought I was the one who was wrong and maybe it wasn't that bad, but now I know it was. I clearly remember the way it made me feel. I felt very alone and that I somehow deserved it. I've spent many of my adult years trying to prove to myself that I deserved it. No matter how successful I am, I don't feel successful. How tragic and unfair. Now through a lot of work on my part, I'm clear that it wasn't my fault and I don't deserve to feel bad. I want to feel good, and this is the start. I've worked on things on my own but now we need to work on a lot of things together. I wish you could have done things differently. I would have loved for you to confront him and tell him if he ever touched me again you would kill him. Or you could have made me feel important and protected - like my feelings mattered! **This is the root of why I seem to scream so loudly; so that my feelings will be heard and understood, because I feel like they never have been.** *I've been made to feel guilty for being sensitive. Well, that's who I am. A beautiful sensitive child who was overlooked emotionally and got things all twisted in my head. Well, they're not twisted anymore. I can't stuff it down and distort my life any longer. Whatever sins of the generations that have been passed down will stop here. I need to speak my truth and live in the right state of mind to raise my children without all the luggage that's been carried around for the last twenty-seven years. I am special. I am important. I am lovable and loving. I am wonderful me.*

The next thing, and I feel the biggest part, was your choice of your new husband. I feel you chose him over me and he was all that mattered. I dropped out of high school and moved out at fifteen because of him. How could you allow your child to do this? Didn't you care? I was entirely too young and still needed you very much. I got love and sex all mixed up. What I really craved was affection, but didn't know how else to get it. You never explained things to me. I wish you could have told me to feel good about myself no matter what anyone thought of me, and that sex is just sex, not love. My young teenage years were so frantic and desperate. I didn't feel I had anything to hold onto. We didn't have God in our lives, the family was split up and the message I got from you was that you were too busy with your own life to take the time to tell me what life was all about. I felt lonely a lot because I've really been completely on my own since fifteen. It's a sad feeling and it makes it hard for me now to let anyone in. It's hard for me to accept help and trust people now. I always feel like they'll let me down, so I don't even give them a chance. My formative years have created this false perception - but now I know that's all it is - a false perception! The truth is that not everyone will leave or disappoint me. This is an important issue I'm still working on - but I will get it...

All those things combined and unresolved over the years have made me feel very distant from you. That's why when I fly off the handle for something small - it's really years of anger and disappointment coming out all distorted.

Let's be real.
What do you have to say?
Love, Annie"

Here is a beautiful illustration of a woman who was so scarred by her childhood wounds that she couldn't see her own worth, her own lovability. When we returned to the Scene of the Crime, she saw where she first learned to devalue herself, to feel unspecial, unworthy, and unimportant. Annie chose to mail her letter, and the process of healing with her mother began.

R.S.V.P.?

Mailing a letter gives the receiver privacy and time to gather thoughts and feelings. There are several different outcomes to these encounters. You need to be prepared for all possibilities:

* **The receiver denies all of your feelings, attempts to invalidate you, dismisses your feelings, and gives you more of the same hurtful behavior.**
* **The receiver ignores your letter.**
* **The receiver becomes severely guilt-ridden and berates her/himself, taking on the role of the victim.**
* **The receiver is able to hear all of your feelings, validates them, and is willing to talk about what happened. Real intimacy and resolution is possible.**

If you choose to write a letter in the course of your own healing, take your time. Think carefully about your Scene of the Crime. Know your Programs. Clearly remember your feelings. Make the connection to your life today. And write about how you wish it could have been. Mail it, keep it, or throw it away. It is in the writing where the feelings are released and the healing occurs.

Homework 7

New Developments

Take a look at your life in **The "Pie" Exercise**. Find the areas that need to be filled in, and add something new. Join a club, start a hobby, development a friendship, participate in a new sport or exercise program, or look for a new job. The goal is to add something new, to reach beyond your comfort zone.

Growth and change often requires the addition of new ingredients.

Insights

_____

_____

_____

_____

_____

_____

_____

_____

_____

_____

_____

_____

_____

"How dear to this heart are the scenes of my childhood,
When fond recollection presents them to view!"

Samuel Woodworth, from "The Old Oaken Bucket" (1785-1842)

Chapter 8

Generational & Cultural Programs

Generational Programs: Politics & Ethnicity

Every decade has its Programs. Rules of child-rearing and attitudes towards family and divorce change from generation to generation, depending on the Programs of the times. During the Depression of the 1920's, everyone felt scarcity and fear. War, the crash of the stock market, and the general atmosphere in the United States gave the **National Programs** of despair, fear, and hopelessness. This created a generational attitude of "wanting, not having." In the 1950's, there was a new **Generational Program**, that of prosperity. World War II and The Korean War were over, and there was an attitude of growth and abundance. These **Political Programs** effected the mentality and psychology of the country, creating a Baby Boom Generation filled with idealism; anything was possible. And when the Baby Boomers grew up and experienced realism, they had to be disappointed. That in turn created another psychological attitude, which instilled new Programs. In the 1960's, Martin Luther King led a nation away from racism towards equal rights for African Americans. New **Ethnic Programs** were installed into the entire country, deleting the old Programs of segregation and discrimination. And because of this, a new time of growth and change began in the United States...

It is important to understand your Parental Programs in the context of Generational & Cultural Programs; not only in your family, but in your Country.

We can break the chain of Negative Generational Programs if we learn to understand how they have been handed down to us. With this understanding, we are free to rewrite our Negative Programs, changing ourselves and generations to come.

Cultural Programs: Environment, History, & Religion

Every country has its own psychology, formed by environment, history, and religion. Environmental influences such as geography and weather have shaped the psychology of entire populations, creating **Environmental Programs.** Historical events such as war and the economy also add to the unique identity of every country on Earth, creating **Historical Programs.** Religious beliefs dictate moral behavior, creating **Religious Programs.** Anthropologists study family customs and rituals to understand social systems. Understanding your heritage can give great insight into your ancestors, and therefore, yourself. For example, the pioneer spirit of The United States of America leads to independent thinking and politics. This differs greatly from Norway, a country which takes care of its citizens under a huge umbrella of socialism; Mother Country. Stereotypes of certain countries are exaggerated, yet based on some reality. Do some research on the nations in your genetic background, and gain some knowledge of the lifestyle, the hardships, and behavior in everyday life. What kind of government was in power? Was it a time of war or peace? Prosperity or hardship? Who was President (or Dictator, Queen...) when your parents were children? What climate did your Grandparents live in as children? Were they wealthy or poor? Were their lives guided by religion, or dominated by political ideology? Look beyond your immediate life and learn about the roots of your family tree.

Limiting Parental Programs

There are many common themes running through Parental Programs. Ideas are often transferred from parent to child, without alteration from one generation to the next. Limitations are often placed unconsciously on children when the parents see themselves as deficient. It is especially obvious when the parent was raised in a different culture or country than the child. Negative or Limiting Programs are glaringly obvious under these circumstances. Ethnic traditions and rituals remain strong, even when the living circumstances have changed due to emigration to a new country with different beliefs. "Machismo" values of some cultures can have a detrimental effect on women in society. Matriarchal and patriarchal values form Parental Programs that continue for generations. Let's look at some typical stories of Limiting Programs due to culture and tradition.

Rosa's Story

Rosa came to this country from Mexico when she was two months old. She has never returned, and yet she feels trapped in the Old World values of traditional Hispanic religious beliefs. Her parents prayed to live in the United States so they could give their children things they could never have. The problem was, they brought their limiting beliefs with them, unconsciously thwarting any growth or success in their children's futures. They programmed what they knew: limitations, stereotypes, and pessimism. Not out of malice, but out of fear and love.

Rosa came to see me when she felt stuck in her Old World lifestyle at the young age of twenty-one. Although she felt proud of her heritage, she longed for the freedom she saw in the American culture. She loved her husband, but he agreed with her parents' Cultural Programs, and she felt trapped.

Limiting Cultural Programs:

"Women stay home and raise babies."
"Men make all the decisions."
" Men are smarter than women."
" A good wife does what she's told."

Going to see a psychologist was already a big step towards breaking the cultural rules of her parents and husband. It took a lot of courage (and secrecy) for Rosa to see me. But she wanted help to break free from the ties that held her back, without breaking the ties to her family whom she loved. She believed their "stereotypical" thinking greatly limited her life choices.

We found the following Programs:

Rosa's Mother's Program:

"You are only a girl, and need a husband who takes care of you. "

"You have to learn how to cook, clean, do the laundry, and take care of your husband and babies because that is your mission in life."

"You are fragile and always sick. "

"You are weak, not born to go to school. "

"You are not pretty. "

"Thank God you are a housewife because you are not smart enough to have a job, not even as a cashier, because that would be too hard for you."

Rosa obeyed her commands by being sick most of the time. She believed herself to be fragile, and her immune system must have gotten the message. She had constant upper respiratory infections and missed a lot of school. She was afraid to even look for a job after graduating from high school, convinced she was incapable of anything. She married, as expected, when she was eighteen, and immediately had two children. Feeling trapped, she defined herself as "just a housewife" with no way out. Her husband actually tried to encourage her to do more if she wanted, but she had no confidence.

In our work together, we looked at her Programs and analyzed which ones were actually true. She had done well in school, despite her Program that she was a stupid girl. Over time, Rosa was able to see her true self. She needed to "get amnesia" to find herself once more.

How Rosa Made Her Programs Come True:

"I am sick most of the time."

"I am afraid to look for a job."

"I am afraid to go to college."

"I am just a housewife."

"I am afraid to speak up to my husband."

Rosa's New Self Programs:

"I want to have a career."

"I want to feel better about my self. "

"I want to feel confident."

"I want to learn how to set goals in my life."

"I want to be happy."

"I want to have the courage to be myself when I am with my family."

How Rosa Will Make Them Come True:

"I will try to convince myself that I am smart and that I have the intelligence to do anything I want in this life. I feel good already about myself because I am able to recognize that I have a problem and I need help to fix it. I will talk honestly to my husband and tell him I do not agree with his thinking. I need to be true to myself and be with someone who respects and supports who I am and how I want to live my life. I was raised as an American, and want to feel all the freedoms of this country."

Rosa will need time to separate her beliefs from her family and their culture. Having been raised her entire life in the United States, she has certain experiences that have shaped her thinking and values. As their daughter, half of her believes in the values and customs of her parent's homeland. The other half is a free-thinking California girl who wants to explore the world. We'll see what happens.

Carrie's Story

Generational Programs are sometimes created during times of war, and yet passed on during times of peace. At the age of twelve, Carrie's mother was taken to a concentration camp in Poland after she witnessed the murder of her entire family by the Nazis. Her tortuous experience during the Holocaust gave her profoundly harsh Programs.

Mother's Historic Generational Programs:

"Life is horrible."
"People are evil."
"It is necessary to fight to protect your life."
"You must fight for everything to stay safe."
"You can never be safe."
"Everything will be taken from you if you are not on guard."
"Life is suffering."
"There is no happiness."
"People are out to get you."

Carrie's mother survived her ordeal and was freed by the Allies at the age of sixteen. She was raised by a family in Europe, married, and moved to the United States. Carrie is her only child. Although Carrie's mother was rescued and went on to live a free and safe life in America, she had received life-long Programs of sadness, fear, anxiety, and anger. And she passed it on to her daughter, not out of hatred, but with love. She felt a need to protect Carrie from the evils of life. So Carrie, born in peace, received Programs of war.

Carrie's Mother's Programs:

"Life is horrible."
"People are evil."
"It is necessary to fight to protect your life."
"You must fight for everything to stay safe."
"You can never be safe."
"Everything will be taken from you if you are not on guard."
"Life is suffering."
"There is no happiness."
"People are out to get you."

Carrie was raised in a crime-free suburb in a house with a white picket fence. Not exactly Auschwitz. But she was taught to feel unsafe, unprotected, and unhappy. Her mother's beliefs were passed down to Carrie by osmosis. She watched her mother's fear, anxiety, pessimism, and sadness. What else was she left to believe, except that life is full of fear, anxiety, pessimism, and sadness. When I met Carrie, she had just been fired from her third job in three years.

Three Times Tells The Truth

If someone tells you something negative about yourself, you may listen, and immediately dismiss it. The person is obviously wrong. Maybe he's having a bad day. Maybe you remind him of someone he didn't like in his past. If someone else comes along and makes the same criticism about you, you listen, and this time you take note. Isn't it curious that another person would have the same problem with you? Hmmmm. But when a third person comes along and makes the same criticism, *now you must listen, take note, and believe them.* This is not a conspiracy. There is no plot to get you. When three unrelated people tell you the same thing about yourself, it must be true. There is a major lesson to be learned here. This is an opportunity, not punishment. Remember, a lesson will be repeated until learned. If you choose to defend and make excuses for yourself, you are not getting it. You will be doomed to go through the same painful experience again and again, until you learn. Listen, and believe.

How Carrie Made Her Programs Come True:

In Carrie's case, she took her Programs to work with her. Because she felt a need to defend her "professional territory," she arrived at her office with a briefcase filled with anger, harsh words, and defensiveness. Her first employer told her she was rude, offensive, and abrasive, and fired her. She thought he was an idiot and got a new job within a month. Her second boss told her she was abrupt, short-tempered, and nasty to co-workers and clients. She thought he was overly sensitive and a "control-freak." But she really admired her third boss, and felt humiliated and embarrassed when he fired her for her inability to get along with co-workers. She couldn't easily dismiss this termination as she had done in the past. Even though she was always given warnings before being fired, she never truly believed her behavior was wrong. Finally, she had to surrender, realizing she must be doing something wrong.

The War Is Over

When Carrie identified her Programs, she quickly saw how she was approaching her life as if she had been in the concentration camp with her mother. Understanding how her mother had unconsciously passed on her own Programs to her, she recognized how ridiculous and inappropriate they were, given her sheltered life in the United States. The worst thing that had ever happened to her in her childhood was that she wasn't chosen to be the lead in the school play. Hardly comparable to starvation and torture. Carrie was able to laugh at herself and her Programs. She wrote new Self Programs, and was able to stop her offensive behavior. She decided to live in peace.

Carrie's New Self Programs:

"Life is safe."
"I am safe."
"There are loving people in the world."
"People are helpful to me."
"I can work with other people."
"People can be helpful, cooperative, loving, and loyal."
"I can be helpful, cooperative, loving, and loyal."

Natasha's Story

Born in the Soviet Union forty years ago, Natasha has seen a lot of political change. Having escaped Communism at the age of ten by moving to the United States with her mother and father, she could not escape the emotional imprisonment of her Generational Programs. It seems that she is reliving both of her grandmothers' lives.

Her paternal grandmother was abandoned by her husband for a career in the Politboro. He believed he could not achieve political greatness with a wife and children. Her maternal grandmother was abandoned by her husband for another woman. He left the family one day without warning, and never returned. So both Natasha's parent's mothers were abandoned, and both raised their children alone. Having witnessed their mothers' hardships, Natasha's parents resolved to make their families the most important part of their lives. And that is exactly what they did. Natasha was an only child, and they made her the center of their being. They had few outside interests, and Natasha felt loved but suffocated by all of their attention. Her parent's anxieties came through with all of their love, and Natasha was left with a feeling of confusion.

Natasha's Parental Programs:

"You are lovable."
"You are everything to us."
"Family is the only thing that matters."
"No one is more important to you than we are."
"We live for only you."
"We don't matter. You are the only one who is important."
"We are the only one's who you can trust to love you."
"Men can't be trusted."

Her Programs were basically very loving, but they came from a place of anxiety and fear. Her parents were witness to their mothers' loss and sadness, and unconsciously passed it on to Natasha. It's as if she received her grandmothers' Programs for loss.

Natasha's Grandmothers' Programs:

"Men cannot be trusted."
"Men will leave."
"You will ultimately be alone."
"Don't trust a man."
"You are lovable, but don't expect to keep a man."
"Men are unavailable."

Natasha made these grandmothers' Programs come true by unconsciously choosing abandoning-men. I first discovered this when I noticed her repeated sentences of, *"How could he choose this over me?"* It sounded so much like what her Grandmothers must have said, so many decades ago.

"How could he choose a political career over me?"
"How could he choose another woman over me?"

When we first met, Natasha was getting over a man who said he loved her but couldn't be with her because he needed to live in Europe to establish his career. He never invited her to join him, although they worked in the same field. He simply cut her off, after an exciting and promising beginning. *"How could he choose his career over me?"*

Her next boyfriend was loving and attentive, and then suddenly told her he was going back with his ex-girlfriend. *"How could he choose her over me?"*

It was as if she was reliving her grandmothers' lives. Her own Parental Programs were loving, but they were created by her parents' in reaction to their own Parental Programs taught to them by their mothers. ***They tried to reject these Programs, but unconsciously passed them down to their own daughter!*** They skipped a generation, and Natasha made her grandmothers' Programs true.

Once Natasha saw the family dynamic, she drew her Genogram and saw the Programs with even more clarity. She saw all of her choices as directly related to her grandmothers' beliefs, and decided to write her own Programs.

Natasha's New Self Programs:

"I can choose to be in a relationship with a man who will be completely available to me."
"There are men who choose love over career."
"There are men who are faithful."
"I deserve to have love and devotion from a wonderful man."
"I do not have to repeat my grandmothers' lives."

The Family Tree

We are all born whole, completely full of self-love and positive beliefs about the world and ourselves. At the Scene of the Crime, the miracle of a child's innocence is turned into self-doubt and damaged self-esteem. No one escapes the hurt and pain of childhood, for no one has perfect all-knowing, all-loving parents. Parents are human. *Parents had parents who were also not perfect.* Our parents had their own Programs which affected their ability to parent us. And on and on and on, generation after generation.

The history of a family tells all, holds secrets, and governs the lives of those yet unborn. One way of uncovering the wisdom of generations is to make a **Genogram.** That's the psychological name for "family tree." It's our lineage, but in more detail.

It's amazing how families tend to regenerate the same personalities, the same problems, the same kind of relationships. Just as some physical diseases run in families, so do psychological dysfunctions. By drawing a Genogram and labeling certain traits, we can gain a greater perspective. Instead of just understanding how we belong in our immediate family, we can understand ourselves within the context of many generations.

Don's Story

Don is a thirty-two year old African American referred by the court and his Employee Assistance Program (See Appendix 4). He had been arrested and convicted for assault and battery after severely beating his wife and putting her in the hospital for several days. The court had given him the option of jail time or probation with psychotherapy. He chose therapy, thinking it would be an easy way out.

During our first session, Don stated that his life had become unmanageable.

"I'm losing everything that's important to me. I got drunk and did this stupid thing. I can't believe I hurt her that bad. I can't even remember doing it. I always knew I had a problem with my temper, but this scared me bad. I want her back. I quit drinking. I want to fix this. I want to fix me. I'm glad I got this chance to work it out instead of jail. But I don't know what to do."

Don is the third child in a family of nine.

"Every year my Mom had a baby. She cleaned houses, worked odd jobs, and we were very poor. My mother was a 'party girl.' She slept around a lot. My father left when I was five, and then I only saw him once in awhile on weekends. But he was real important to me. And when I was ten, he died of a heart attack. I didn't handle that too well. I was real depressed, didn't go out, didn't talk to anybody, didn't go to school. I just remember that I always wanted to run away after that. I played Superman, pretended I could fly away. I ditched school, started drugs and alcohol when I was thirteen. I really got bad when I went into the Navy at eighteen. It just kept getting worse and worse."

Just prior to our meeting, Don had been in an in-patient alcohol treatment center for five weeks, and attended AA meetings for the first few weeks. He had since stopped, stating he had no need for them and couldn't relate to others in the group.

"Something happened to me when I got arrested and saw what I had done to my wife. It's like the desire to use drugs and drink has been lifted. I know you probably hear that a lot, but it's true."

At this time, I encouraged Don to return to AA, at least three times a week. Alcohol and drugs are powerful, and addictions need to be treated with respect. As they say in AA, *"If you are not working your program, you are going backwards."* You can't stand still and expect to grow.

Don is presently a sales representative for a large company. Although he has been in this field for about six years, he has moved from one company to the next. The longest time in one job had been eighteen months. He states that he likes the freedom of his own hours and schedule, and often takes several days off per month. But his bosses in the past have always pressured him to produce more, causing him to quit and move on. He admitted to earning just enough to get by, and didn't understand why he had no ability to get ahead.

Don had been married for three years after an unstable courtship of two years. He had two children with his wife, ages three and one, and another seven year old from a previous girlfriend. He admits to never having had a monogamous relationship, and believed himself and all men to be incapable of fidelity. *"We men have different needs than you women."* Having been raised in a matriarchal society, he believed it was normal that the grandmother raises the children, the mother is absent, and the father is never around. Sadly, this is still quite prevalent in the African American community, although great progress has been made through community efforts and education, like the Million Man March on Washington. But Generational Programs die hard.

Don always behaved in a very seductive manner towards me. When I confronted him about this, he at first denied all intentions, then later admitted that he tries to seduce all women, mainly out of habit. He thinks this is his role as a man. He thinks women expect it from "real men." He was especially attracted to white women. He said he had never had a relationship of length or importance with a black woman.

"I think it has to do with the fact that my mother was so promiscuous. I guess I just don't trust black women in general. I probably don't trust any of you. I saw my mother with a different guy every night. I didn't know she was a prostitute at the time."

Underneath his outer mask of charm and wit, Don was mildly depressed and anxious about his feelings of anger and lack of control in his life. He admitted to feeling confused and helpless.

"I'm worried that my wife will file for divorce. I know I don't love her like a man should love a wife, but I don't want to lose her. I'm not used to feeling bad. In the past, when I felt like this, I'd just get high. Now, I just feel it all and it's hard."

Much of the therapy was in our relationship. I, as the therapist, represented "all women," and he expressed great curiosity about my marital status, sexual activity, and history. He knew nothing about my personal life, which left him free to form his own impressions about my values. He went to great lengths to seduce me away from the "therapist" role to a "girlfriend" role, wanting to "conquer," but yet always respecting my boundaries. I believed that he unconsciously thought that if I could keep my boundaries intact, then maybe women in general could be trusted. For example, when he first started to think of going back to his wife, he became extremely concerned about her ability to be faithful to him, stating that all women sleep around. He then asked me questions about my own ability to be monogamous. The conversation was turned back to focus on his feelings of abandonment. How would he feel if she were unfaithful? Again, he would hypothesize about my sexual activity. It would be during these times that a moment of insight would take place about his own fears and pain. He would choose to be the "cheater" rather than the "cheated on." His macho exterior made it difficult for him to articulate his inner feelings about fears of betrayal. I learned over time that whenever he focused on my sexual activity or became curious about me in my relationship, he was unconsciously expressing his fears within his new relationship with his wife. Later, when I pointed this out to him, he saw the connection. Our relationship evolved into one of trust which translated into an ability for him to eventually trust his wife.

Don's Scene of the Crime

If we look at the Scene of the Crime, we see a promiscuous mother who was emotionally absent, a part-time father who eventually abandoned Don through divorce and death, and a family setting of nine children raised by a grandmother. Don was lost in the crowd, and taught that he was unimportant, undeserving of love and attention.

Don's Mother's Programs:

"All women are promiscuous."
"Women will betray you."
"Women are not there for you."

Don's Father's Programs:

"Men are not responsible for their families and children."
"Men leave."
"Men are unfaithful."
"If you allow yourself to really love someone, they will abandon you."
"Men are not responsible for their families."

When Don was able to see that his beliefs about women and family were based on these Programs, he recognized everything he had unconsciously done to make his life repeat his forefathers' Programs. We drew his Genogram, and he saw how he took his place with all the men who battered their women, abandoned their wives and children, and escaped with alcohol and drugs. We don't know how many generations this goes back, but Don knew it would stop with him.

His progress was steady and positive, and after one year of weekly therapy, his criminal record was erased. He continues to be clean and sober. He has reconciled with his wife and they are in marital counseling. His mother has received therapy for herself during the past two years, and they were able to resolve many of their past issues during a recent visit. Don's income and productivity on the job continues to steadily improve, and he has been able to save money for the future purchase of a condominium. Don has joined the "thirty-something" crowd.

Don's
GENOGRAM

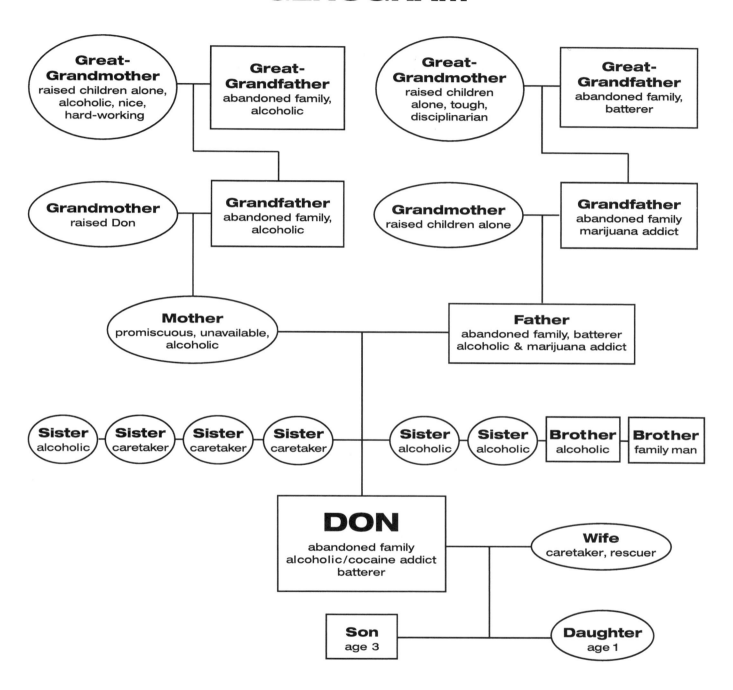

New Self Programs:

Recovering Alcoholic, Faithful Husband, Devoted Father, Good Provider

The Generational Programs have been deleted, changed and Positive Programs
will be passed on to Don's children, and to their children, and on and on...

Your Turn

Questionnaire 8: Whose Life Are You Living? will help you find your place in your family history. *The "Genogram" Exercise* will give you a tangible, historic blueprint. And *Homework: Tell Me A Secret* will add to your family knowledge.

Questionnaire 8

Whose Life Are You Living?

1. Who is your favorite relative?

_____

_____

_____

_____

2. How are you like that person?

_____

_____

_____

_____

3. Is there a history of alcohol, cancer, diabetes, heart disease, or any other medical problems in your family?

_____

_____

_____

_____

4. Do you worry that someday you will have this problem?

_____

_____

_____

_____

5. Describe the different personalities in your family,
   including your grandparents.

_____

_____

_____

_____

6. Do you take after anyone in particular?

_____

_____

_____

_____

7. Describe the educational levels of your family. What were your **Educational Programs?**

_____

_____

_____

_____

8. Did you equal or exceed these levels? Did you choose another path?

_____

_____

_____

_____

9. Describe the work and professions in your family, as many as you can. Get a picture of the **Professional Programs** in your family tree.

_____

_____

_____

_____

_____

10. Did anyone in your family influence you towards the work you do?

_____

_____

_____

_____

11. Describe the financial situation in your family history.
Was there excess, just enough, or debt? Find your **Financial Program**.

_____

_____

_____

_____

12. Do you feel comfortable in the lifestyle you have? Do you live with
excess, just enough, or in debt?

_____

_____

_____

_____

_____

13. Are the marriages in your family life-long? Are there divorces? Are there multiple marriages?

_____

_____

_____

_____

14. Are the families large, small? Do the families interact often? Are there family feuds or rifts?

_____

_____

_____

_____

15. Is there a feeling of extended family?
Does most of the family live in the same city or state?
Is the family scattered? Are there family reunions and activities?

_____

_____

_____

_____

The "Genogram" Exercise

Purpose: * *To identify family patterns and traits*
           * *To understand yourself within the context*
             of generations

Using the Genogram in Don's story as a guide, draw your own Family Genogram. Go back as far as you can, enlisting the help of older family members for details, dates, and family stories. After you have written in all the names in the boxes, (square boxes for men, circles for women), draw a line through all deceased family members, noting their age at the time of death.

Add in the health history. You can abbreviate, if you'd like. Next to each box, for example, write an "A" for alcoholic, "C" for cancer, "D" for diabetes, etc. You may also define each person with a descriptive adjective next to their name. Capture the essence of the personality, health, and lifestyle of each family member.

Make the Genogram as elaborate and detailed as you want. After it is complete, find the person most like you. Who has similar Parental Programs? Discover if you are re-living someone else's life, another relative's Programs. Notice how Programs are passed from generation to generation. Do you want *your* Programs passed down to future generations? By changing yourself, you can make a difference for centuries to come.

Homework 8

Tell Me A Secret

Contact a relative who knows a lot about your family history. It could be your older sibling or a favorite aunt. Get a new perspective on your parents and their parents. Your childhood memories are limited because you had the intellect of a child. Often, I will hear a childhood story that's been told over and over again, whether it makes sense or not. Sometimes, if something sounds confusing or sense-less, I am aware that it's probably a story learned in childhood. It's now necessary to step back and look at our lives through adult eyes.

Ask questions, look for new explanations for things that have never made sense, or that you've always wondered about. Learn and see what really happened with adult eyes.

New stories often shed new light on old stories.

Insights

_____

_____

_____

_____

_____

_____

_____

_____

_____

_____

_____

_____

"...And forgive us our trespasses, as we forgive those who trespass against us."

from The Lord's Prayer

"Only the brave know how to forgive... A coward never forgave; it is not in his nature."

Laurence Sterne, from "Sermons, vol.1" 1760

Chapter 9
Tools for Recovery

Feelings of powerlessness, defenselessness, and hopelessness are emotions well-known to victims of low self-esteem. We watch as they move from one dysfunctional relationship to another, from abusive partners to neglectful marriages. We watch them in their feeble attempts to recover from one trauma, only to enter into another drama. And all of this abuse is seen by them as further proof that they deserve this treatment, that they somehow cause it. We recognize our friends, acquaintances, family members (and ourselves?) as they endlessly repeat this negative behavior.

If we were taught at the **Scene of the Crime** that we are worthless and deserving of abuse, we will take this **Program** into adulthood and make it come true. We will be attracted to the exact dysfunctional person who can abuse us and make us feel unworthy, less than, and unlovable. It is as if we have sensitive radar with an uncanny ability to scan huge numbers of people, able to by-pass those who would love us. Instead, we zero in on just the right person with whom we can re-enact our trauma from childhood.

And then something wonderful happens. We hit bottom. We cannot take another moment of neglect, abuse, or pain. We admit we've had enough. We stop letting it be OK to feel miserable and we reach out. To a therapist. To a friend. To a church. To a book. To a trusted teacher. And lights go off and bells ring and **we finally get it**! But now what? We don't have a clue as to what to do instead. We try to get out of our hurtful relationships. We try to do what healthy people do. We meet nice people, people who treat us with respect and love and care. And we feel out of place, awkward, uncomfortable, bored, and undeserving.

And so we read self-help books, enter therapy, and/or join a 12-Step Program, and finally begin our personal road to recovery. We actually begin to focus on ourselves, realize our own likes, dislikes, needs, and dreams. But we still don't totally know how to "do it." How do we learn to be in a healthy relationship without losing our newly found sense of self?

We need tools to live life as worthy, lovable, hopeful, and complete men and women. We are taught science, reading, math, art, and history. Nowhere are we taught about human relationships, emotions, parenting, or how to interact.

Children in relatively healthy homes are taught that they deserve to speak their minds, to have input in their relationships with one another. They see loving role models of male-female interaction. They are treated with love and respect, and are therefore taught to treat others with love and respect.

But what about those men, women, and children from abusive homes, from dysfunctional homes, who are not given the necessary messages and role-modeling on how to live happy, productive lives? Where do they learn?

Psychology School

I strongly believe, and hope, that psychotherapy will be part of the educational system in the future. Children could be seen once a week in group settings, or individually, based on need. They would be taught the art of being healthfully human. *We could deal with each child at the time of the Scene of the Crime.* Someday, human relationships will be a topic of study in elementary school.

But today, we must turn to learning these skills in healthy living from books, therapists, 12-Step-Programs, and from allowing ourselves to be in loving relationships.

If you are not presently in therapy, but have become curious and interested after participating in this Workbook, I urge you to seek out a competent psychologist or psychiatrist. **Appendix 4** lists referral sources to help you find someone suitable. Make sure the person is licensed and has good references.

Transcendence

It is rare, but once in awhile, I meet someone who refuses to believe their Parental Programs, even at the Scene of the Crime. Sun is a perfect example. She always knew that her parents were wrong and saw herself through her own positive eyes, despite what her parents were teaching her. She felt she had been born into the wrong family, and did everything within her power to remove herself from the dysfunction as soon as she was able. She overcame her Limiting Programs and transcended her circumstances. It's as if she wrote her own Programs while she was still a child, and made them come true.

Sun's Story

Sun looked like one of those beautiful Asian women in the James Bond films. Exotic, elegant, and very sophisticated. You would never guess her childhood circumstances or her Parental Programs. That's because she refused to accept them, even as a small child. I have seen this a few times. Somehow, at the age of three or four, Sun remembers thinking that her parents were wrong. Amazing. She saw through the abuse and believed herself to be a wonderful little girl living in the midst of chaos. Growing up in Japan with an alcoholic father and a suicidal mother, Sun spent many childhood afternoons planning her escape to the United States.

Sun's Father's Programs:

"You are a bad girl."
" You deserve to be beaten."
" You are worthless because you are only a girl."

Sun's Mother's Programs:

"You deserve abuse from your father."
" You make my life miserable."
" I have no time for you because you are unimportant."
" You make me suicidal."

But, Sun wrote her own Programs:

"I am lovable."
"I am living in the wrong family. "
"I am worthy of love."
"I will find love in the United States where I can be free."

As soon as Sun was old enough, she escaped using a brilliant plan which I promised never to divulge. It took courage, confidence, intelligence, and self-love. I respect her very much for her ability to take care of herself, in spite of such an abusive childhood.

Once in the United States, she educated herself while working full-time. With an advanced degree, she became very successful in her chosen career. She has a loving husband and is expecting her first child.

Inner Tools

Growth and change are processes that will continue for the rest of our lives. We have liberated ourselves with New Self Programs, and have deleted old Negative Programs. Our eyes have been opened, and we will never close them again. There's no going back. This is not to say that our old dysfunctional ways of thinking and behaving are gone forever. We learn, make progress, and sometimes slip back into comfortable, negative behavior. Work is needed to remain vigilant and mindful, paying attention to our choices and actions every day. Know that you may always have a weakness that needs to be watched. It is yours to overcome, conquer, and cure.

The Stories, Questionnaires, Exercises, and Homework in this book offer practical methods to make our recovery easier and happier. I also suggest using the following tools:

* **Honesty & Integrity**
* **Trust**
* **Self-Knowledge**
* **Assertiveness**
* **Kindness**
* **Defenselessness**

* **New Programs**
* **Fight Fear**
* **Act As If**
* **Risk**
* **Self-Talk**
* **Goal Setting**

Honesty & Integrity

If we have lived most of our lives in unhealthy relationships, most likely we're not accustomed to living in honesty. We have lived in the denial of our own emotions, needs, and feelings. We may have integrity when it comes to our dealings with others, but we need to treat ourselves with the same respect. Ask someone just out of a bad relationship where she would like to go for dinner and she will say, *"I don't care, wherever you want."* She has no idea about her own opinions. Her focus has not been on herself. She has not honestly addressed her self. Often, we're under so much stress that we don't take the time to know if we're OK. We tell others *"I can handle it,"* only to collapse with the flu or a migraine. **The body doesn't lie.** We lie when we say we're OK, but the body contradicts. Our body will make us sick in order to make us stop, to make us truthfully see ourselves.

Be honest. Don't deny when something is wrong, just because it feels easier. Whenever you feel that pang in your stomach or solar plexus, trust it. Something is wrong. That's the truth. When someone does something or says something that gives you that "gut" feeling, your body is telling you the truth. Something is wrong. Be honest. Being politely passive and agreeable are no longer options. Tell the truth. Live with integrity.

Trust

Abusive relationships teach us to not trust what we see. We learn to see the danger in every situation, in every relationship, in defense of our selves.

We learned to distrust, because disappointment is intolerable and surprise is dangerous.

And yet, in healthy relationships, trust is essential. We trust the person in relationship with us is real, good, kind, honest, and forthright. And in order to trust the other, we have had to learn to trust our own judgment. This takes time. We need to prove to ourselves that this time we have chosen to open our hearts to someone who will treat us with love and respect. This time, we will love someone who will not betray us. It is often ironic that when we meet a loving person who is deserving of our trust, we cannot recognize them yet. Our healthy radar is not yet trusted. The war is over but no one told us. We're like soldiers still armed for battle, and the rest of the world is waiting for us to feel the peace. Trust is a process that can be learned by facing the fear, by trial and error.

Self-Knowledge

If we were raised in abuse, the focus was on "other" and not "self." It was necessary to pay close attention to the mood and behavior of others in order to protect ourselves emotionally and/or physically. We sometimes didn't have time to know own feelings and needs and wants.
Today, if we're not aware of who we are as individuals, we will continue to be lost. We know that feeling. Lost, unimportant, not special, not worthy. Always attentive to the needs and desires and whims of others, always the perfect audience. But true emotional health requires self-knowledge. We need to be whole, complete, aware, fully-functioning men and women in order to connect with others in a healthy way.

Assertiveness

There is a whole spectrum of behavior that runs from passive to aggressive. Passive is the victim who allows the abuse. Submissive, apologetic for her own existence. Silent responses to hurtful behavior in hope that it will go away. Aggressive behavior is the violent, and just as inadequate, coping mechanism in response to the same hurtful behavior. Physical violence, emotional abuse, and verbal assaults. But there is something in the middle, in the place of balance. Assertiveness.

Passive   Assertive   Aggressive

If you see two people at a distance in an argument, the one who is yelling and animated is losing.

Imagine two people in an argument. You can see them but you can't hear their words. One is animatedly gesturing, appears to be yelling, and is making severe facial expressions. The other person has relaxed facial features, and appears to be calmly speaking in a normal voice when it is her turn. The first person is losing the argument.

When we feel frustrated, hopeless, unheard, unimportant, and desperate, we think that it will help if we speak louder, meaner, harder, faster, and more. And when we feel powerful, heard, certain in our truth, our feelings, our desires, we can speak in a **quietly powerful** way, and other people are able to hear it without needing to defend, without feeling attacked. We speak our truth. **Attack-lessness. Defense-lessness**. Just the truth.

We use "I" statements, telling calmly how "I" feel, not accusatory "You" statements which illicit defense from the other person. We quietly powerfully tell the other what it is that hurts us or makes us angry.

"I feel hurt when..."
"I don't like it when..."
"I want you to stop..."
"I feel angry that..."

And we offer alternatives.

"I would like it if you..."
"I want you to ..."
"I want to..."

If we are attacked, we know our individual rights as human beings and feel able to calmly discuss our disagreements, knowing we are quite capable of protecting ourselves from harm in any way.

I cannot stress the importance of reading and re-reading a good assertiveness training book. It is one of the first steps in recovery from abusive relationships. **Know your rights as healthy women and men.**

Learn how to assertively express yourself in a quietly powerful way. Remember the **Quietly Powerful Rules** in Chapter 2. It is possible and necessary to retain a strong sense of self within the context of a relationship.

Be assertive. That means you know yourself, understand your needs, and speak up, so sometimes you get what you want, and sometimes you get your own way. Take your own inventory. Know your likes and dislikes. Never say *"I don't care"* if someone asks what you'd like for dinner. Make something up. Start to care. Have an opinion, but don't be opinionated. Express yourself, your desires, and preferences. Assertive behavior means freedom and entitlement.

Kindness

Mostly, what we are trying to learn is simple kindness. Respect, courtesy, tactfulness, gentleness. Practicing kindness in all our encounters adds sweetness to our lives. And if we do it at home, we will find new meaning in old relationships. If we can grow and change in just one way, let it be in becoming kinder. It embodies all of the traits we need in order to live a happy, successful, and fully self-actualized life. Remember, **K.I.S.S. means Kindness Is So Simple.**

Defenselessness

In the Martial Arts, one is taught to get out of the way of the aggressor. If someone is attacking you, it is best to move off to the side, thereby letting the attacker fall down under the momentum of his own strength. Defenselessness. It seems counterintuitive, but if you choose to strike back during an attack, there will be a meeting of two forces, each made weak by the other. If, on the other hand, you choose to not join in the battle, but to merely get out of the way, it takes away the power of the aggressor to hurt you, and points out the violence of his behavior. I'm not talking about physical abuse here. I'm describing a way of emotionally going through life. If someone rages at you, speak back in a Quietly Powerful way. (See Chapter 3). If someone expresses aggression towards you, get out of the way. Leave, make yourself safe. Reassess the relationship. Wait until things are calm to express yourself. If someone cuts you off in traffic, let them. They will get there fifteen seconds before you do. If a stranger is rude to you, smile and wish them a nice day. A defense with anger is perceived as an attack by the aggressor, which calls for a counter-attack, and on and on. Choose your battles with wisdom, and know that they are few.

New Self Programs

Remember, the coping mechanism you used as a child which worked well then is the very behavior that is hurting you as an adult. Look at the following chart and see how New Self Programs and coping skills are important for your new life of freedom.

Adult Situations, Child Solutions

Childhood Situation	Child's Feelings	Child's Coping Technique	Results (Good)
Neglected Unloved Uncared for or Abused	I am: Unlovable Inferior Not-good-enough Undeserving sad	Passive Blends in Quiet Stays invisible	Less punishment Receives some care Safer

Adulthood Situation	Adult's Feelings	Adult's Coping Techniques	Results (Bad)
Wants relationship but...	Same as child's (see above)	Same as child's (see above)	Fear of relationships True-self unseen Alone
Wants good job but...	Same as child's (see above)	Same as child's (see above)	Holds self back Takes no risks Doesn't try Stagnant Stuck Unsuccessful Seen as having no ambition

Situation	Old Program Feelings	New Program Coping Techniques	Possible Results
You are asked out on a date.	I am: unlovable, inferior not-good-enough undeserving sad	Fight fears "Act as if" Risk Self-Talk: New Self-Programs Trust	Friendship Relationship Experience Self-Esteem +
You have a job interview.	I am: inferior not-good-enough undeserving	Fight fears "Act as if" Risk Self-Talk: New Self-Programs Trust	You get the job. Experience of the interview. Self-esteem +
You are criticized.	I am: wrong bad inferior not-good-enough	Fight fears "Act as if" Risk Self-Talk: New Programs Trust	Self-esteem + conflict resolved

New Program Coping Techniques

Fight Fear:

I will no longer allow my fear of losing someone to cause me to reject them first. I will fight the fear. It's better to be afraid than to be alone.

"Act As If":

I will "act as if" I already believe that I am lovable, deserving, good-enough, and worthy of someone's attention.

Risk:

I have learned that it is better to play, to speak, to be myself, than to hide, keep quiet, and worry what others think of me. I need to risk being myself, or else be alone.

Self-Talk:

I remind myself of my New Self Programs. I remember who I am.

Trust:

When people tell me they care, I believe them. They are telling the truth.

Goals

If you don't like where you are, you need to go somewhere else. Before you can go somewhere else, you need to know where you want to go. You will go where you are looking. Find out where you are looking. Set goals. But keep them flexible because you don't know what your choices will be in the future. Just have an idea of what you want to do, where you want to go, and what you wish to accomplish.

This Week's Goals

_____

_____

_____

_____

This Month's Goals

_____

_____

_____

_____

This Year's Goals

_____

_____

_____

_____

Future Goals

_____

_____

_____

_____

Steps I Need To Take For This Week's Goals

_____

_____

_____

_____

Steps I Need to Take For This Month's Goals

_____

_____

_____

_____

_____

_____

_____

Steps I Need To Take For This Year's Goals

_____

_____

_____

_____

_____

_____

_____

Steps I Need To Take For Future Goals

_____

_____

_____

_____

_____

_____

_____

Your Turn

Questionnaire 9: Who Do You Want To Be? points you even further towards identifying with your New Self Programs. *The "Guilt" Exercise* will free you from the unnecessary burdens of a useless emotion. *The "Stay In Pain" Exercise* allows you to feel and express your true self in times of stress. *The "Acceptance" Exercise* gives you a new way of dealing with everyday problems. *Homework 9A: Dream* will free you to believe you can have what you want. And finally, *Homework 9B: Pass It On* will strengthen your growth and change.

Questionnaire 9

Who Do You Want To Be?

1. Who is your favorite film star? What do you admire about this person?

_____

_____

_____

_____

2. Who is your favorite literary character? Why?

_____

_____

_____

_____

3. What one trait do you admire most in others?

_____

_____

_____

4. What are your best qualities?

_____

_____

_____

_____

5. What do other people like about you?

_____

_____

_____

_____

6. What don't you like about yourself?

_____

_____

_____

_____

_____

7. What have other people criticized about you?

_____

_____

_____

_____

8. How would you change your personality?

_____

_____

_____

_____

9. What prevents you from doing so?

_____

_____

_____

_____

_____

10. What bothers you about other people?

_____

_____

_____

_____

11. What situations get on your nerves?

_____

_____

_____

_____

12. How would you like to manage your life better?

_____

_____

_____

_____

_____

13. Is there anything you would change in your living conditions?

_____

_____

_____

_____

14. Is there anything you would change about your relationships?

_____

_____

_____

_____

15. Can you imagine being content with your life if it stayed the same?
    Can you imagine being content with your mate and job as they are today?

_____

_____

_____

_____

16. What do you need to do to make yourself a more accepting person?

_____

_____

_____

_____

_____

_____

_____

_____

_____

_____

_____

_____

_____

The "Stay in Pain" Exercise

Purpose: * **To be aware of authentic pain and feelings**
** * To learn how to speak from the heart**

When someone hurts us, we naturally go into a position of defense. If someone is mad, we immediately feel scared of being wrong, rejected, or unloved. We automatically defend, *even when we're wrong*. It's hard to trust that when someone is angry with us, they can still love us at the same time. And so our defense takes the form of attack.

We need to learn that someone can be angry at our behavior and still love us. We can be angry at someone's behavior and still love the person.

This takes trust in ourselves and in the relationship. The next time you're hurt by your mate's behavior, **stay in pain**. Anger is an easier, less painful emotion than sadness, and so we go there easily. Instead, I am asking you to feel the hurt and sadness, and speak from that place in your heart.

"I feel hurt by what you said."
"I am so sad that..."
"I feel disappointed that..."
"I am depressed because..."
'I am scared that..."

Your mate will be able to hear your pain and will naturally want to comfort you or clear up the misunderstanding. If you speak from a place of defensive anger, you are essentially in a position of attack, and the other person then needs to defend against you. An argument begins. Instead, **stay in pain.** It is authentic, real, and direct. The issue will be resolved with more understanding and ease.

The "Acceptance" Exercise

Purpose: *** To let go of the need to control relationships**
         *** To learn how to accept others as they are**

How many of us live in a world of pretense without awareness? How many of us prefer to see things the way we wish they were, rather than as they are? Acceptance of the truth brings inner peace and happiness. Denial brings forth anger and disappointment.

Most of us have pre-conceived ideas of how a husband, sister, mother, son, or best friend *should* behave. We have a rigid picture of each category. This is what a husband looks like. This is what a sister does. This is how a mother acts. This is how a son should talk. This is how a best friend should be. And so when we meet the *real* person, it's as if we close our eyes so we don't see the parts of them that don't conform to our perfect picture. We then hurt them with our anger, our disappointment, and with our tirades of how much they are not how we want them to be.

See-Accept-Forgive-Release-Decide

Most of us act surprised when someone behaves in character for them but out of sync with how we want them to act. **Surprise implies expectation.** We expect instead of accept. We hope instead of accept. And we punish instead of accept. We're often in a state of denial. It's absurd and ridiculous to pretend that people are the way we want them to be. And yet that's exactly what we do. We get amnesia and actually act *surprised, angry, and dissapointed* when they act in ways that irritate and annoy us.

So how do we change from critical, judgmental expectation to unconditional acceptance?

First, we must learn to *See* others as they really are, in the light of day, with our eyes wide open. We take away the "wishful thinking" lens and actually see the person. This can be quite a shock, especially if we've been lying to ourselves about who someone really is. It takes practice because we prefer to see just the good. But we must see all of the person, even the bad parts that don't conform to the ideal person in our minds.

Secondly, we must *Accept* what we see as the truth. This is the essence, the inner core of the person. This is the character; the good, the bad, and the ugly. No one is all good, no one meets all of our needs and desires, no one is who we want them to be completely. It's sad, but true. And we need to accept that.

Next, we **Forgive** them. We forgive them for not being perfect, for being less than what we want, for being too much in other areas. We forgive them for being human, and for having character defects.

Then, we **Release** them. We release them to themselves, to the universe, to God, to whatever we believe in. We let them go. We allow them to be whoever they are. We release them to be on their own path of life and growth. It's not our job to fix them, to judge them, or to criticize them. They are individuals, separate from us, with their own lessons to learn, *in their own way, in their own time.*

And finally, we **Decide**. Given that we have seen who they really are, accepted them for who they are, forgiven them for not being all we want them to be, and released them; we decide. We decide who we want them to be in our lives. The way they are. Not if they change. Just the way they are. Now.

If we truly go through these steps, daily, with every person in our life, we will feel peace and acceptance. We are allowing others to be themselves without negativity, judgment, or blame. We are not the police. We accept those whom we decide we want in our lives. We surround ourselves with loving people, and choose to let go of the bad. By allowing others to be who they are, we are giving the gift of acceptance. When others sense that we have let go of our controlling, critical agendas, they feel freer to be themselves, and are more loving in return. You get what you give.

How Do I Do This?

Let's look at some examples of this exercise. The following are simple everyday occurrences that make us angry, hurt, annoyed, disappointed, and generally dissatisfied with our relationships:

Problem #1: Your husband is chronically late, and each time you react with anger.

Solution #1:

"I see that my husband is usually half an hour late for everything. I accept that. I forgive him for not being on time like I am. I release him to live on his own timetable. I have decided to make allowances for his lateness. If we have a 7 p.m. dinner reservation, I will tell him that I would like to be there at 6:30. I'm not asking him to change, but I won't be frustrated by his lateness either. I just plan on it. This satisfies my need to be on time, and doesn't depend on changing him. If I need to be somewhere important and I see he will not be on time, I will leave without him, giving him the option to join me later, or to not come at all."

Problem #2: Your brother is self-absorbed and tends to talk of nothing but himself, and you continue to feel hurt by his lack of concern for you.

Solution #2:

"My brother just called and told me all about his latest job promotion and never once asked about me and the kids. I recognize he is limited in his capacity to give to others, and I accept this, although it's difficult and disappointing. I forgive him for not being the brother I wish I had. I release him to learn to be more loving, but I can't be the one to teach him. I have decided that I don't turn to him when I need a good listener. Instead, I tell him things about the family that he might be interested in, realizing his gifts lie elsewhere. I accept him for who he is."

Problem #3: Your father is a chronic worrier and never fails to point out the negative in any situation, and each time you are annoyed by his comments.

Solution #3:

"I see my father is a worrier, and I can accept that about his personality. I forgive him for not being the father I need him to be. I release him to learn to let go of fear, but my yelling at him will not do it. I have decided that I can't tell him about real events which may cause him worry. I expect him to point out the dangers involved in topics we discuss. I no longer try to reassure him that everything is safe and will be OK. He never believed me anyway. Instead, I listen to his concerns and say things like, 'That's true, that's too bad, I'll be careful...' and gently move on to another topic. I accept his fears and anxieties."

Problem #4: Your son is focused on sports to the exclusion of everything else and you are continually frustrated with his "I don't care about the family" attitude.

Solution #4:

"I see that my son is going through a normal teenage stage of self-discovery and self-absorption. I miss him and wish he would participate in the family, and I hope he will in the future. I forgive him for being ego-centric. I release him to the strange world of adolescence, to grow and become an individual. I have decided that if I want to have a nice talk with my sports-fan son, it will not be by nagging him about homework. I can accept that his passion for sports is normal and part of his development, and I can willingly support him at his games."

Problem #5: Your best friend has asked your advice on the same problem for years, but never follows any suggestions. She repeats the same painful mistakes over and over again, and you feel powerless to help her.

Solution #5:

"I see that my best friend needs someone to listen to her while she gathers the strength to take action. I forgive her for not learning sooner. It's not up to me to decide what's good for her. I do not judge her. I detach and give her support. I release her to learn her own lessons, in her own time. However, I have decided to limit the time I am willing to invest in listening to her problems. I am not in this world to devote my time and energy to other people's problems. I refer her to a good therapist, knowing I can't give her what she needs."

A lesson will be repeated until learned.

Accepting ourselves and *our own* shortcomings is often the most difficult thing we can do. Most of us repeat the same mistakes until we finally get sick of the same consequences. Time to grow and change. The ***Acceptance Exercise*** is not easy, quick, or ever complete. It is an on-going process. It takes constant mindfulness, discipline, and fortitude. And as with any exercise, it gets easier with practice. The rewards in your relationships will be great. The alternative is what you've been doing until now. Acceptance versus judgment. Choose.

Perhaps in our quest for spiritual growth, we will continue to look inward to free and heal ourselves first. The rest will follow . . .

Homework 9A

Dream

Sometimes we forget to wish for what we want. I often hear about the problems and the fears, but rarely do I hear about the dreams and the wishes. When I ask, *"What do you want? What would you like to happen?,"* the answer often is, *"I don't know."* How can we improve our lives and gain happiness and healthy relationships if we don't have goals? I don't believe in setting goals with rigid timelines. We can't know what are choices are five or ten years from now. But I do recommend having present and near-future goals to strive for and achieve. But first we have to dream. Children dream and wish all the time. It's a natural instinct that somehow gets extinguished as we mature.

Go back to a child-like state and dream, and wish, and set new goals. Let yourself be wild. Having bland dreams and safe wishes is unexciting and non-motivating. What do you *really* want?

You end up where you are looking.

Be specific. If you want a relationship, describe the kind of person you're looking for. Where do you meet? What do you do together, where do you go? If you want a new career, write about the details of the job. What are your co-workers like, what's your salary? Are you self-employed? Are you wearing a suit or jeans? Use your imagination. Make a dream list and keep it nearby. Daydream and wish everyday. And then do the work.

Homework 9B

Pass It On

The best way to own a new behavior or way of thinking is to teach it. As your friends and family notice your newly-found sense of freedom to be your true self, they may ask you what changed in your life. Teach someone you care about the ideas you have recently learned. Pass it on.

Insights

_____

_____

_____

_____

_____

_____

_____

_____

_____

_____

_____

_____

_____

Afterwords...

The Beautiful Restaurant

The beautiful restaurant sat high atop a hill at the end of a winding mountain road, overlooking a lovely seaside village, nestled in the green valley below. A very hungry woman was driving in her car, on her way to the beautiful restaurant. She had heard stories that this was the most delicious, nourishing, romantic restaurant in all the world. She was told the food melted in your mouth, the waiters catered to your every need, and it felt special just to sit at the beautiful tables with fine china, linen, and silver. But she was very hungry because she hadn't eaten for many days. She hadn't taken care of herself because she was too busy taking care of everyone else. And so she wondered if she had the strength to reach the beautiful restaurant atop the hill at the end of the winding mountain road, overlooking the lovely seaside village, nestled in the green valley below. Along the way, she saw lots of other places to eat. Fast-food restaurants, diners, little restaurants, fancy restaurants. All seemed to be beckoning to her. She felt tempted to stop for a small bite to eat, just to satisfy her until she got to her destination. But if she stopped, she knew she would spoil her appetite and delay her arrival. She knew that she was already late. She felt tempted to give up completely, to simply stop to eat her dinner in one of the other restaurants, because she feared she would starve to death. She began to doubt whether she had enough gasoline in her car to reach the beautiful restaurant. She wondered if she remembered the directions. She felt so lost and hungry. But she decided to continue on her way, strong in her resolve to settle for nothing less than the beautiful restaurant atop the hill at the end of the winding mountain road, overlooking the lovely seaside village, nestled in the green valley below.

But she persisted, and when she finally arrived, she was greeted by a handsome valet who escorted her to the maitre d' who seated her at the most exquisite table with beautiful people, next to a warmly lit fireplace. The waiters brought her the finest food on the most elegant china and she ate until she could eat no more. And she was happy.

Moral: Only You Can Determine The Quality Of Your Life.

Appendix 1

Audio Tape for Relaxation

"BREATHE...
AS IF YOUR LIFE DEPENDED ON IT" ©

Based on progressive relaxation techniques, this 30 minute audio tape gently guides you into a state of peaceful serenity. Dr. Cairns' soothing voice, words, and original music allow you to release emotional and physical tension.

"Breathe...As If Your Life Depended On It" has been used to successfully assist in the treatment of anxiety, insomnia, headaches, panic attacks, phobias, and depression.

ANXIETY   Helps calm and soothe
with gentle words, calming voice, and beautiful music.

INSOMNIA   Helps gently relax you into sleep state.

HEADACHES   Helps ease tension in head and shoulders.

PANIC ATTACKS Helps reduce fear of losing control by centering
attention inward.

PHOBIAS   Helps calm fears by focusing on
internal sensations.

DEPRESSION   Helps return attention to self in the present time.

You may use Dr. Cairns' relaxation tape on a daily basis. Listen to it after a stressful day, or anytime you want to feel better; sitting in a comfortable chair, or in bed as you drift off to sleep.

$10 plus $2 shipping

VISA Orders: Fax 310.246.9545 or Tel 310.858.7474
(Please include VISA Card Number, Name on card, & Expiration Date)

Check or money orders:
Life Goes On Productions
Dr. Kathleen Cairns
Post Office Box 18380
Beverly Hills, California 90209

California residents: please add 8.25% State tax (83¢)

Appendix 2

A Simple Meditation

Come inside your quiet self,
a place of peace and serenity...

Quiet your mind.
Turn off your thoughts.
Go inside.
Everyday.
Once a day.

Your special time...

Find a **quiet peaceful** place in your home.
Make a space for yourself...

Surround yourself with sun, **warmth**, beauty;
Your sofa, a pillowed-chair...
Make yourself **comfortable**.
Anywhere...

Sit with straight spine,
Head **rests easily** on your neck.
Arms are at your side or in your lap.
Feet on the floor or cross-legged...

Let go of every muscle.
Relaxed body...
Relaxed mind...

Close your eyes.
Do nothing.
Notice your **breath**.
In and out.
In and out.
In
and
Out...

Notice thoughts come in and out.
Return to your **breath**.

In and out.

Notice your **breath**...

Deeper
Now shallow
Slower
Now faster...

And **transcend** to
No thought.
No breath.
No where.

Away.
Transcended.
Peace and serenity...

20 minutes each day.

Every day.

Bliss...

Appendix 3

Breathwork

**Useful to lessen physical symptoms of
anxiety and depression**

Exercise 1. Abdominal Breathing

1. Breathe through your nose.
2. Inhale slowly, pushing your abdomen out, letting the air
    gently fill your lungs.
3. Expand your chest, letting it fill with air, fully and completely.
4. Hold 5 seconds.
5. As you exhale, draw in your abdomen, pushing out the air from your lungs.
6. Repeat 10 times.

Exercise 2. Rhythmic Breathing

1. Inhale slowly and rhythmically through your nose for a count of 8,
    filling your lungs deeply and fully.
2. Hold for a count of 8.
3. Exhale slowly for a count of 8.
4. Hold your breath for a count of 8.
5. Repeat 10 times.

Exercise 3. Cleaning Lungs Breathing

1. Breathing through your mouth, blow out air from your lungs by quickly
    contracting your abdomen in sharp bursts. Do 60 in one minute.
    If you feel dizzy, slow down.

Exercise 4. Panting Breathing

1. Pant like a dog with your mouth open and your tongue relaxed.
2. Count to 100.
3. Breathe in and out at the same speed as when panting, but this time,
    keep your mouth closed and breathe through your nose.

Appendix 4

Referral Sources for Psychotherapy

Employee Assistance Programs (EAP)

An Employee Assistance Program (EAP) is a mental health benefit offered by many companies in the United States, Canada, and parts of Europe. Counseling is offered to all employees for assessment and referral regarding any personal problem. There is no fee to the employee for 3-10 sessions, depending upon the contract in a particular corporation. Total confidentiality is assured. Referrals are made to resources in the community for psychotherapy, medical treatment, marital counseling, financial advice, attorneys, and crisis centers. The company may have their own in-house EAP therapist, or choose to contract with a private EAP. Over the years, companies have learned it is cost effective to invest in the mental health of their employees. It has resulted in more efficiency, reduced absenteeism, and happier, more productive employees.

Physicians

Your Physician or Primary Health Care Provider should be able to refer you to a competent therapist in your area.

Hospitals, Crisis Centers, Clinics

Hospitals, Crisis Centers, and Clinics often have excellent therapists who may work on a sliding scale; they may base your fee on your ability to pay, according to your income and expenses. Check your community yellow pages.

Pastoral Counseling

Churches, synagogues, and other religious organizations usually offer counseling to their members. Often the priest, minister, or religious leader has received training in personal and family issues.

Friends and Family Members

If you have a friend or family member who has benefited from counseling, you may want to ask them for the name of their therapist. It can be reassuring to receive a referral from someone who has already been helped by this person.

Appendix 5

Suggested Readings

I often give reading assignments to my patients to speed up the process of learning, growth, and change. Reading between sessions stimulates the mind and brings the therapy into your everyday life. I offer the following list from books I find to be most helpful. Some are new, and others are old classics. I also recommend that you browse the psychology and self-help sections of your bookstore or library. Sometimes, a title will jump out at you, and may be just what you need.

Asserting Yourself by Sharon Anthony Bower & Gordon H. Bower
The Anxiety & Phobia Workbook by Edmund J. Bourne, Ph.D.
Co-dependent No More by Melody Beattie
The Courage To Heal: A Guide For Women Survivors Of Child Sexual Abuse
        by Ellen Bass & Laura Davis
A Course In Miracles pub. by Foundation For Inner Peace
Dance Of Anger by Harriet Lerner, Ph.D.
Embracing Each Other by Hal Stone, Ph.D. and Sidra Winkelman, Ph.D.
Getting Him Sober by Toby Rice Drew
Getting To 'I Do' by Pat Allen, Ph.D.
Healing The Shame That Binds You by John Bradshaw
Honoring The Self by Nathaniel Branden, Ph.D.
Hypericum & Depression by Harold Bloomfield, M.D.
Intimacy & Solitude by Stephanie Dowrick
It Will Never Happen To Me by Claudia Black
Love Is Letting Go Of Fear by Gerald Jampolsky
Love, Medicine, & Miracles by Bernie Siegel, M.D.
Making Peace With Your Parents by Harold Bloomfield, M.D.
Men Are From Mars, Women Are From Venus by John Gray, Ph.D.
A Natural History Of The Senses by Diane Ackerman
Peace Is Every Step by Thich Nhat Hanh
A Return To Love by Marianne Williamson
The Road Less Traveled by M. Scott Peck, M.D.
The Seven Spiritual Laws Of Success by Deepak Chopra, M.D.
Sick & Tired Of Self-Improvement? by Barbara Barnett, Ph.D.
Solitude by Anthony Storr
What Smart Women Know by Steven Carter and Julia Sokol
When Bad Things Happen To Good People by Harold Kushner
Women's Bodies, Women's Wisdom by Christiane Northrup, M.D.
Women Who Love Too Much by Robin Norwood
Why Weight? A Guide To Ending Compulsive Eating by Geneen Roth

ABOUT THE AUTHOR

Kathleen Cairns, Psy.D. is a Licensed Clinical Psychologist and Certified Hypnotherapist with a private practice in Beverly Hills, California. For the past twenty-five years, her work has focused on the teaching and development of communication and intimacy skills in relationships. Her areas of expertise include anxiety and depression, recovery from addiction, adult children of alcoholics, agoraphobia, stress management, the mindbody connection, and death and dying.
Dr. Cairns is a consultant to Project Nightlight, an organization dedicated to helping AIDS patients without families in the final stages of dying. She is also affiliated with several national corporate psychology organizations. Dr. Cairns has conducted seminars in Los Angeles and Hartford based on the "Parental Program" model. She has appeared on national television and radio talk shows.

For phone consultations and counseling, you may contact her at 310.858.7474.

TO THE READER

I hope that by participating in The Psychotherapy Workbook you have identified your own Parental Programs and have learned a lot about yourself. I would love to hear from you about your self-discoveries; your Scene of the Crime, your Programs, the ways you lived by them, and how you've changed your life now by writing new healthy Self Programs. I would like to include your story in a sequel to this book.

Letters will be kept confidential, and I will respond to all. Thank you.

Please write to me at
Post Office Box 18380, Beverly Hills, California 90209
or
e-mail lifegoeson@earthlink.net

Book Order Form

_____

_____

To order more copies of
The Psychotherapy Workbook @ **$14.95 plus $3 shipping per book:**

VISA Orders: Fax 310.246.9545 or Tel 310.858.7474
(Please include VISA Card Number, Name on card, & Expiration Date)

Check or money orders, mail to:

Life Goes On Productions
Dr. Kathleen Cairns
Post Office Box 18380
Beverly Hills, California 90209

California residents please add 8.25% State sales tax ($1.24)

Name: _____

Address: _____

             _____

             _____

Tel/Fax   _____

VISA Card Number   _____

Name on card   _____

        exp date   ____/___

#___ Book(s) Ordered: $_____
CA Sales Tax: _____
Shipping: _____

Total: $_____